A Healer In Every Home
Dogs & Cats

A Healer In Every Home
Dogs & Cats

Begabati Lennihan, RN, CCH
Margo Roman, DVM
Shirley Moore

GreenHealing Press   Cambridge, Mass.

GreenHealing Press
777 Concord Ave. Suite 301
Cambridge, Mass. 02138
www.greenhealing.org

Discounts on multiple copies are available by ordering from our website. We make the book available inexpensively in bulk to enable veterinary practices and shelters to provide it to their clients. Individuals are also welcome to receive a discount when ordering two or more copies.

ISBN: 978-0-9834430-1-8

Cover design: Ron Frank

Front cover photo by Deborah Grady of Katy Nichol,
    Dr. Margo Roman's vet tech, with Marnie and Lottie

Back cover photos:
    Dr. Margo Roman, photo by Simone Hnilicka
    Shirley Moore, photo by Dave Bernier
    Begabati Lennihan, photo by Dr. Lydia Knutson

Disclaimer: It is advisable to seek the guidance of a veterinarian before implementing the approach to health suggested in this book. It is essential that any reader who has any reason to suspect that an animal suffers from a serious illness check with his or her veterinarian before attempting to treat it with this method. Neither this nor any other book should be used as a substitute for professional veterinary care or treatment.

Acknowledgements: The information in this book is based on studies with Dr. Richard Pitcairn and Dr. Luc De Schepper and on books by Dr. Don Hamilton, Dr. Patricia Jordan, Christopher Day, Allen Schoen, Barbara Fougere, Kaetheryn Walker, and many others, as well as on our own experience with animals.

Dedication

To the animals who are our teachers

Hi there! Thanks for joining us for the "animal companion" version of our popular **Healer In Every Home** book for families.

I know a lot of people will be buying both books, so I'm trying not to repeat myself in this one. If you'd like to enhance what you read here, please check out our first book, for people. You'll be surprised at how many remedies you can use for both animals and people!

For this book, I have two special co-authors: Dr. Margo Roman and Shirley Moore, both of whom studied at my homeopathy school.

Margo Roman is a remarkable holistic vet who incorporates acupuncture, chiropractic, homeopathy, herbal medicine, and nutritional supplements at her practice (MASH, Main Street Animal Hospital of Hopkinton, Mass.). Margo is a pioneer in holistic veterinary practice, for example as the first woman vet trained in acupuncture. She founded one of the first integrative clinics in the US in 1993, and here she shares the fruits of her vast practical experience with animals.

Shirley Moore is remarkable in a different way. She has saved thousands of dogs who would otherwise have been euthanized by founding a humane society, Save A Dog in Sudbury, Mass. (more information at www.saveadog.org) After her own dramatic cure with homeopathy, she started using holistic methods with the dogs in her shelter. The result? Healthier and happier dogs, plus she saved her nonprofit tens of thousands of dollars a year in vet bills.

Not only that, she has empowered hundreds of volunteers and adoptive dog-parents to use the simple methods in this book. If they can do it, you can too!

– Begabati Lennihan, RN, CCH
Cambridge, Mass.
May 22, 2011

This book is a simple, user-friendly introduction to holistic health care for your pet. Once you try out the methods in this book and discover how easy they are, we'll guide you to the best of the more advanced books, in the **Resource** section in the back.

We'll get you started with the basics . . .

o   a healthy diet

o   minimizing medications

o   the best of herbs and special natural remedies called "homeopathic remedies"

As you may know from our first book, homeopathy ("home - ee - OP - uh - thee") is a very safe, fast-acting, gentle yet powerful form of natural medicine found in every natural food store and easily available online. But it's rarely used because people just don't know about it.

So we're about to change that – we the authors plus you the readers, trying this on your pets, being amazed by the results (we hope), telling your friends . . .

So let's get started with this healing adventure.

You'll be glad you tried it. The results will be worth it:

o   You'll save lots of money on health costs over your pet's lifetime

o   Plus you'll save on time spent at the animal hospital

o   And best of all, you will enjoy a more peaceful and playful pet.

Sources of products

You can get most of the remedies recommended in any natural food store.

The rest can be easily obtained online, for example at
www.homeopathic.com
www.elixirs.com

And this is probably a good place to mention that the authors have NO financial interest in any of the products recommended.

A note about word choice:

We use the word 'pet' for your animal, with apologies to those who find the term demeaning. 'Animal companion' best describes our relationship with our domestic animals but was too clunky to keep repeating in this book.

We sometimes use 'animal caretaker' or 'parent' to mean the human responsible for a domestic animal, and 'adoptive parent' for those who provide a permanent home for an animal rescued from a shelter. 'Foster parents' are those who take animals home from a shelter temporarily while permanent homes are found. Mostly, we're avoiding the word 'owner' which doesn't come close to describing the relationship we have with our pets

Also, we mostly talk about dogs and cats, but the same remedies are used for all furry creatures. Actually birds and reptiles respond well to these remedies too! And amazingly enough, the same dose works for everyone from a chinchilla to a horse, because these energy medicines work by transmitting information to the body's healing energy – so quantity does not matter. More about this in our first book, *A Healer In Every Home: QuickStart Guide.*

Contents

Let's Get Started 1

Your Home Remedy Kit 2
   First Aid Remedies 2
   Basic Directions for Homeopathic Remedies 4
   Pre- and Post- Surgery 6
   Accidents and Traumas 9
   Wounds 11
   Quick Tip: Green Tea and Hydrogen Peroxide ... 12
   Splinters, Creaky Joints 13
   Cruciate Ligament Problems 14
   Bee Stings 15
   Hives and Kennel Cough 16
   Dog Bites 17

Animals Have Feelings Too 20
   Flower Essences for Emotional Healing 27
   Calming a Barking Dog 28
   Calming an Overly Aggressive Dog 29
   Calming a Dying Animal 30

Your Pet's Personality 33
   Animals and Their People 39

Raw! Raw! Raw! 41
   Fallacies About Raw Food 42
   Switching to a Raw Foods Diet 44

Tummy Troubles 52
   Vomiting 52
   Diarrhea 53
   Possible Poisoning 53
   Abdominal Instructions 55
   Preventing Hairballs in Cats 58

Ear Problems - Listen Up! 59
    Food Allergies...59
    Ear Mites 61
    Remedies for Ear Infections............................62
    Chronic Ear and Skin Problems.......................64
    Hot Spots 65

Ticks and Fleas – the Mighty Bites 66
    Fleas and Avoiding Toxic Flea Repellents...........66
    Ticks: Get a Grip..69
    Intestinal Parasites and Heartworm 71

Rabies – The Original Vampire Story 72

Vaccines – Hold That Shot! 76
    Ideal Minimum Vaccine Schedule 79
    Realistic Minimum Vaccine Schedule 80
    Minimum Vaccination Schedule for Kittens 82

Talking to Your Pet 83

Rescue Tales from Save A Dog 87

Resource Section 95
    New Dog Instructions.....................................96
    Holistic Protocol for Shelter Dogs 103
    Directions for Mixing Homeopathic Remedies 106
    How to Give a Pill to a Cat 109
    Quick Guide to Homeopathic Remedies 110
    Why Give Probiotics to Dogs 111
    FAQ Sheet on Lyme Prevention......................112
    Lyme Prevention with the Lyme Nosode 116
    Natural Dewormer 118
    Recommended Reading 120
    Recommended Suppliers................................124
    Recommended Websites 125
    Find a Practitioner 126

About the Authors..127

Let's Get Started

Before we start, here are the guiding principles on which this book is founded:

1. **Use natural remedies first.** Following the doctors' adage "First do no harm," start with safe natural healing methods. Use pharmaceutical drugs only as a last resort.

2. **Feed raw foods and give good supplements.** Try to make your pet's diet as close as possible to what they would eat in nature. Hint: dogs and cats didn't evolve by opening cans!

3. **Minimize medications and vaccines.** Most pets are way over-vaccinated, leading to cancer and other chronic illnesses. Give the absolute minimum vaccines necessary to keep them protected against serious illnesses (and to comply with the law, in the special case of rabies).

4. **Find an integrative vet** – you may have to travel a distance for one of these very special vets trained in holistic modalities – so you'll probably need to find an open-minded conventional vet nearby for routine visits. (See www.ahvma.org for a directory of holistic vets.)

5. **Respect your pet as a conscious being.** Try to imagine what life feels like from your pet's point of view. Don't get angry or punish your pet for behavior that is natural for its breed. Most pets are subject to environments that are totally unnatural for them – inside a house and alone most of the time. Find ways to make your pet happy in its own doggy way or kitty way.

6. **Learn to listen to your pet** – they are much more aware than we realize and they have their own ways of communicating to us. Listen – and you will learn.

Your Home Remedy Kit

First Aid Remedies

For first aid we use homeopathic remedies because they work so fast! You can get these in any natural food store or online (www.homeopathic.org), and it would be wise to keep the main ones on hand. (They're not the same as herbal remedies – they look like little white pellets, and they come in a tube with a long Latin name. Here we'll use their nicknames.)

When your pet is first injured, you'll probably use one or all of these top remedies:

Aconite if your pet is frightened – for example, just hit by a car. We often give a dose of Aconite first while on the way to the animal hospital, then move on to …

Arnica for the actual injury – bruises, soreness, swelling from soft tissue trauma. Animals need Arnica a lot!

- o just fell from a balcony or deck
- o got into a fight with another animal
- o rambuctious running, slammed into something
- o birds that fly into a window or windshield

It will reduce the pain, swelling and inflammation, and sometimes prevent a trip to the animal hospital. But if you're not sure, don't take a chance – go to the vet!

Calendula is for anytime the skin is broken: cuts, wounds, lacerations – let's say your dog steps on broken glass and has a bleeding paw pad. Calendula prevents pain, infection and scarring and knits the sides of the wound together.

Story Time

A Golden Retriever came limping into Dr. Margo Roman's office recently, having just been hit by a car. Margo instructed the owner to dissolve 3 pellets of **Arnica** 30c (the strength or potency) into 4 ounces of water, then put it into a sports bottle. The owner then squirted it onto the dog's tongue and the affected leg, and applied a cold compress.

Within an hour the dog was walking just fine and seemed to be out of pain. Dr. Roman determined that further diagnostic tests and treatments were not necessary.

Arnica saved the owner a lot of trouble – and a lot of money!

But of course you should take your animal to an emergency animal hospital if there's a possible broken bone or other serious injury. You can always give remedies on the way to the hospital. And you might need to make the remedy stronger – see instructions on the next page.

Try to get **homeopathic Calendula** for emergencies - if you can't find it in a store, get it online. Dissolve 3 pellets in 4 ounces of water to both squirt in your animal's mouth and pour over the wound. You can also soak a gauze dressing with Calendula water.

Next best – herbal Calendula, easily available in natural food stores as a tincture or external application. The homeopathic form is more effective if you can get it.

Basic Directions for Homeopathic Remedies

You can put a few pellets onto your pet's tongue.
Food in the stomach doesn't matter – you just want a
"clean mouth" (nothing else in it). It's okay to get them
inside the cheek next to the gums.

*(PS If you can't get the pellets out of the tube, hold it vertically
with the clear plastic lid on the bottom and twist the cap
firmly, which will pop a pellet out with each twist. You might
need to peel off the little paper sealing strip, or it might come
off when you twist the cap.)*

It's not always easy to get the pellets in, though!
So we use the **squirt method**, especially for dogs.
Cats don't like to be sprayed or squirted, so when my
cat is asleep I tuck the little pellet inside her lip.
She sleeps most of the time anyway!

For larger dogs you can use a **sports bottle**,
for smaller dogs a **syringe** that you can get at any drug
store, the kind used to give medications to babies.

For homeopathic remedies, the bottle or syringe has to
be clean and never used for any other remedy.

For herbs and essential oils it doesn't matter – you can
mix different herbs and oils in the same bottle –
but homeopathics need a clean bottle.

The standard potency or **strength is 30c**, which is what
you'll find in any natural food store (unless otherwise
noted in this book).

The standard mixture is **3 or 4 pellets per 4 ounces**
of water; better not to use tap water if you have a
choice. Distilled or spring water is better.

If you'll be using it up right away, no need to preserve it.
But if you want to keep it on hand, add a little clear
alcohol such as **unflavored vodka, or vegetable**

glycerine, available in drug stores. Flower essences are best preserved with peach brandy (see page 27).

So once you have your mixture, you can squirt it into your pet's mouth. If the teeth are clenched, it doesn't matter, just as long as it **touches the mucous membranes**.

In fact, if you can't get it in the mouth, try applying it to the **ears or paw pads** – it will absorb through the skin.

Quick Tip: Making It Stronger

In a real emergency situation, you need to make the remedy strong enough to keep pace with the intensity of the symptoms. Suggestions:

o   Give it more frequently - every 15 minutes

o   Succuss the bottle a dozen times or more – giving it hard whacks against the palm of the opposite hand

o   If you have an accident-prone pet, keep **Aconite**, **Arnica** and **Phosphorus** on hand in a 200c (stronger) potency. You'll need to order this potency online–it's not in stores.

More about these remedies on the next page . . .

Pre- and Post-Surgery

The same remedies are used for surgery as for first aid –
plus another handy remedy:

Phosphorus is used both for the effects of anesthesia,
and to control bleeding. (Use it for other bleeding
situations too - nosebleeds or nails trimmed too short –
don't feel bad, this happens a lot!)

Arnica helps control the pain after surgery, prevents
bruising, and increases circulation to the surgical site to
help your pet heal faster.

Calendula closes the surgical incision, helps it heal
quickly, and prevents infection and scarring.

Here's another amazing thing Calendula can do, in Dr.
Roman's experience – usually after surgery the whole
digestive system shuts down, but Calendula gets it going
again right away!

Even after spay surgery (potentially painful surgery to a
female dog's abdomen), Dr. Roman finds that painkillers
usually aren't necessary when using homeopathy. That's
great, she says, because these conventional medications
have side effects and can delay healing.

Your pet's comfort is the most important thing, though.
Don't hesitate to give painkillers if you can see that the
remedies just aren't strong enough.

So here's what you do:

Give a squirt of Arnica into your pet's mouth before
surgery, and bring Phosphorus for your vet to give during
surgery. Explain that Phosphorus is to prevent bleeding
and the after effects of anesthesia.

Afterwards you need Phosphorus *only* if your pet is bleeding heavily, or to reverse the effects of anesthesia if they are taking too long to wake up. Usually you discontinue it and start the Arnica right after surgery.

If there is lots of trauma after the surgery, use a higher potency of Arnica (200c is the next highest strength – see previous page).

Calendula is used afterwards instead of antibiotics, unless there's a lot of infection. It can be both squirted into the mouth and applied topically.

Bellis perennis is one more remedy to use: it's special for abdominal surgery when the internal organs have been manipulated a lot.

Spay Surgery

Staphysagria is a special remedy to use after spay surgery – it's an especially vulnerable area, and an animal that is already frightened and insecure, such as a rescue animal, may feel traumatized after spay surgery. Staphysagria will help.

Dental Surgery

Silica is a remedy to use for gum irritation after dental surgery – in addition to our old favorites Arnica, Calendula and Phosphorus, which prevent pain and swelling after an extraction.

Hypericum, the remedy for nerve pain, is used if your pet seems to be in pain after a dental extraction.

Use Calendula in a little water to rinse the mouth after dental cleaning or dental surgery.
Hint: this also works for **bad breath in dogs**!

Orthopedic Surgery — fractures too!

Symphytum and **Calc. phos.** are the remedies we add when bones are involved. They reduce pain and speed healing by 30%. You'll need to order these high potencies online:

Give Symphytum 200c once a day for 3 days,
then Calc. phos. 200c once a day for two weeks,
and make sure there's adequate calcium in the diet.

Ruta grav. if the bone is bruised, when there seems to be lots of pain in the bone itself.

More Tips for Your Home Remedy Kit

Back to **accidents and traumas**:

Be careful not to get bitten. If your pet is injured, he may not recognize you, panicking from pain and fright. **Aconite** will help calm him down so you can handle him safely.

If your pet has been bitten and you don't know the source of the bite, handle him with leather or rubber gloves. If you're not sure, it's best to assume there could be saliva from a rabid animal on your pet – which could be deadly for you.

You also want to make sure your pet can breathe okay. If not, get her to the emergency hospital right away – and on the way give **Carbo veg.**, another important first aid remedy.

Carbo veg. has the amazing ability to **promote oxygenation** – in other words, it can help move oxygen from the lungs to the bloodstream to the cells. This could save your pet's life!

You can use it anytime an animal has difficulty breathing:

- o asthma
- o congestive heart failure
- o collapsed trachea
- o weak, can't resuscitate them

Rescue Tales from Save a Dog

We had to do spay surgery on a 12 year old dog. Normally you would never do a spay surgery on such an old dog, but humane societies are required to spay or neuter all adult dogs prior to adoption.

That same night, the dog was gasping for air and it looked like she was going downhill fast – I thought she was going to die.

I put a few pellets of **Carbo veg**. on her tongue as there was no time to mix it up in water.

It calmed her down right away, she stopped gasping, and this simple remedy saved the dog's life.

– Shirley Moore

Wounds: use Calendula, like we already talked about, to heal them up quickly without pain or infection.

BUT – here's the big BUT with Calendula – sometimes it works too well!

Let's say it's a **bite wound or other deep puncture wound** (stepped on a nail, for example). Calendula can heal the top layer of skin too quickly, while there's still infection underneath.

So we don't start with Calendula. We use **Ledum** instead, the best remedy for puncture wounds, until the wound can heal from the inside out.

First, clean the wound well with hydrogen peroxide to bubble out any debris or hair. (It's really important to get hair out of the wound, because hair will prevent healing.)

Then soak it in green tea: see the directions on page 12 for hydrogen peroxide and green tea.
Then use **Arnica** for two days,
Ledum for two days,
then **Calendula** until it's healed,
all of them in a 30c potency three times a day.
(30c is the standard potency available in natural food stores.)

If it's a superficial wound, you can start applying Calendula topically right from the first day.
For deep wounds - wait until the deepest part is healed.

Keep the wound protected for 72 hours with a light gauze bandage to make sure your pet doesn't lick it. But then you have to be careful your dog doesn't eat the bandage! Or use an Elizabethan collar. (You know, those funny cone things that fit over a dog's head and make it nuts because it can't reach an itchy spot!) Or if it's on the dog's back, put on old T-shirt for when it rolls on its back.

Quick Tips: Green Tea and Hydrogen Peroxide

Green tea is not only good for you – it's great for your animal pal as well! Steep 3 teabags in a cup of hot water, then use it as a soak, say for a bite or puncture wound, to open up the wound (once the tea has cooled off enough). Or if you just need a little, steep one teabag in 1/3 cup of water.

It's also great for **cleaning a pet's ears:** soak a cotton ball in green tea, and if they're really gross, squeeze some drops of green tea into the ears to loosen up the wax and debris. Your pet will probably shake her head pretty hard – honestly, it will probably make her kinda crazy to feel water in her ear. So make sure she doesn't mess up your clothes or your place. Maybe do it outside!

You can also use it for the **eyes:** after steeping the teabag, squeeze it out and use it as a compress. Dipping it back and forth into the brewed tea will contaminate the brew, if there's debris or gunk in the eyes. So use a tissue at first to get the gunk out, then use the teabag as a compress.

With the eyes, it's extra important to make sure the tea is not too hot.

Hydrogen peroxide is just water with extra oxygen in it. Totally safe! When you pour it on your pet's wound, the extra oxygen bubbles out and carries with it debris from the wound.

You can use it full strength on a small wound and dilute for a large area or if it seems to sting the animal. If it stings your pet could react; make sure no one gets bitten or scratched.

To dilute: use distilled water, or boil water to purify it, then let it cool before mixing in the hydrogen peroxide.

More First Aid Tips

Splinters or pieces of glass in the paw pads:

o **Homeopathic Silica** will push out foreign objects.

o Sometimes soaking the paw pad first with warm
   green tea will help soften it up so the Silica can
   work. And if there are tiny pieces still left,
   hydrogen peroxide may bubble them up and out!

Creaky joints: when older animals get stiff in the joints,
or playful younger ones get a sprain or strain, try

o **Rhus tox.** if your pet is slow to get up, then shuffle-
   shuffles, then starts to move better;

o **Bryonia** if your pet really seems to be in pain with
   the slightest movement.

o **Chiropractic** can help pets as well as people!
   Puppies play rough and can get out of alignment, so
   it's important for puppies to have several adjustments
   along the way as they "grow into their frame."
   For older dogs it can help realign the skeleton and
   help joints heal faster.
   And for any injured animal, chiropractic can help
   heal faster because it helps the nerves function
   properly. Hit by a car? Definitely take your pet to a
   chiropractor.

o And of course **nutritional supplements – vitamins
   C and B$_{12}$** plus supplements like **glucosamine,
   chondroitin, boswellia, curcumin, and ginger.**
   Don't worry, you don't have to memorize this long
   list – there are combination formulas for
   joint problems that include these nutrients.

Cruciate ligament problems

This is what happens when a ligament tears in your dog's knee. It's a huge problem in dogs, especially ones that lack a solid foundation – ones with poor nutrition, over-vaccination, misalignment of the neck and pelvis, and early spay or neutering.

> **Important note:** Did you know it's important to delay spay/neuter surgery because the hormones are so important for bone growth?

Any dog can rupture a cruciate ligament if they are *injured.* It's the dogs in poor health that get *spontaneous* ruptures, like when they're just playing ball.

So if you have a dog that was spayed/neutered early, be sure to get chiropractic adjustments until its spine is well-aligned, and also be sure to feed raw food and avoid over-vaccinating.

And if your dog has one cruciate ligament tear, it's extra important to follow these guidelines (chiropractic adjustments, raw food and minimal vaccines) – to speed healing of the first ligament and to prevent reinjury.

Once a dog has had one cruciate ligament injury, there's a high likelihood of another one.

Remedies to heal the ligament:

o **Arnica, Ruta grav., Rhus tox.** and **Calc. carb.** are all good candidates - try rotating them to see which one works the best.

o **Calc. carb.** is especially likely to work in a Calc. carb. dog - see page 34.

o **TurmericForce by New Chapter** is an excellent way to reduce joint inflammation. See the story on p. 45.

o **Acupressure** is a wonderful way to help relieve pain in many areas, especially joints, and connect with your pet at the same time. Learn the specific points for each problem in Cheryl Schwartz' book *Four Paws Five Directions.*

o **Laser light** can be used on the acupressure points. Get a laser pointer, the type used for PowerPoint demonstrations, and spread your pet's fur so that the red light shines on the acupressure points for the area you want to heal. It doesn't get hot and won't hurt your pet.

o This is a new variation on Traditional Chinese Medicine which Dr. Roman finds effective. Note that the acupuncture points for a given organ or limb are often in an entirely different part of the body.

But it's also helpful to laser the "ouch point" — the actual point of pain or injury.

More about this system at www.marciazais.com.

Bee Stings

These can be serious, even deadly – see the story on page 92. Shirley Moore says she always carries **Apis** – "don't leave home without it!"

Shirley says that many times when people call her while their dog is reacting to a bee sting, she tells them to stop at Whole Foods for Apis 30c on the way to the vet. They put a couple of pellets of Apis on the dog's tongue, and a lot of times the swelling has gone down by the time they get to the vet!

Hives

o **Apis** is likely to work anytime there is swelling or water retention or a raised bump. Try it for edema or cystitis, or for swollen eyelids when your pet has conjunctivitis.

o **Apis** is the most likely choice – if that doesn't work, try **Urtica urens.**

Kennel Cough

At Save A Dog, Shirley uses **grapefruit seed extract** in the dog's food as it not only prevents and cures giardia, but it shortens significantly the duration of kennel cough. She has been able to get rid of kennel cough in as few as three days just with grapefruit seed extract alone. Remember this is not grape seed extract, but grape**fruit** seed extract.

The beauty of it is that the tablet is brown colored and looks like kibble so you don't even have to disguise it. Think of a 125 mg tablet or a big Lab and cut it down for smaller dogs.

Dr. Roman uses **Source Naturals Wellness Formula** or **First Defense,** plus homeopathic remedies:

o **Spongia** if your pet has a sensitive tickle in throat. with some difficulty swallowing,

o **Antimonium tart.** if it's a barking or honking cough,

o **Phosphorus** if it's a Phosphorus type (see page 33)

Dog Bites

What do you do when the dog bites *you?*

Use the same remedies as for an injured animal - usually **Arnica and/or Ledum**.

For bites or injuries in a nerve-rich area, use **Hypericum**, described in the next two stories from Shirley Moore.

Rescue Tales from Save A Dog

One time when Shirley was studying homeopathy, she got bit in the hand by a frightened dog. Her first thought, as she ran for her kit: "puncture wound." It's something we teach in the first weekend of homeopathy school!

Then she thought "nerve-rich area" because it was in her hand, where there are a lot of nerve endings, and which was in excruciating pain.

So she alternated **Ledum**, for puncture wounds, with **Hypericum**, for wounds in nerve-rich areas. A volunteer offered her **Calendula** and she said no, because it was not a clean wound. (There's a danger that Calendula will work so fast and so well, it will heal the surface skin over a deeper infection.)

She alternated Ledum and Hypericum every 15 minutes for several hours, then every hour for the rest of the day. The wound was so bad she debated whether to go to the ER for stitches but decided to wait until the next day – it was so well healed that she clearly did not need stitches!

Rescue Tales from Save A Dog

Shirley took in an older bloodhound, a huge 120-pound dog named Mugsy. He was in such pain he could hardly walk because the children in his previous family would ride him like a pony. He seemed lame so she tried the typical back pain/ joint pain remedies, **Rhus tox.** and **Ruta grav.** They provided temporary relief but did not cure.

In this type of situation – when remedies relieve temporarily but the condition keeps relapsing – we have to consider whether there is an underlying pathology. Shirley took Mugsy to a vet hospital, where surgery was recommended. But this would be expensive for the owner and traumatic for Mugsy, who was 6 years old – already an advanced age for such a large dog.

Shirley suspected a nerve damage because of all the trauma to his spine. So she took Mugsy to an orthopedic specialist for a full workup. The first thing the specialist did was to lift Mugsy's tail. He yelped with pain. "Neurological damage," the specialist declared. "Yes!" said Shirley to herself.

She told the owner to use **Arnica** and **Hypericum**: Hypericum on a daily basis for the nerve damage and Arnica after coming in from a walk or run, for any soreness.

Six months later she ran into Mugsy's owner. "I have a brand new dog!" he exclaimed. Mugsy was running in the woods and wagging his tail, activities which were impossible earlier when Mugsy was in pain.

Shirley says this story is a great example of "slow and steady" healing. Sometimes, especially with an older dog or a long-standing condition, you have to be patient. She finds that owners tend to give up on homeopathy too soon and run to the vet for cortisone.

But if they stay with homeopathy, they are likely to get complete recovery with minimal trauma for their beloved companion.

Animals Have Feelings, Too

Our first homeopathy teacher, Dr. Luc De Schepper, was fond of bringing in advice columns from the newspaper, and of pointing out that a homeopath could give much better advice.

One woman wrote in that one of her two dogs had died, and the other one seemed to be moping around and refusing to eat. The advice? "Get another dog to keep the first dog company."

As Dr. Luc said, "The dog misses the other dog, and another dog wouldn't be the same! If her husband died, would the solution be to get another husband?"

Dr. Roman adds, though, for some dogs getting another dog would be perfect. Some dogs, like people, grieve too long and need distraction. Some dogs want a buddy in the household, while others want to be the "only child." Some pets will become more confident and "step forward" in that situation. So you have to be sensitive to your pet's needs.

Animals respond emotionally to a wide range of situations:

o   the death of a family member or another animal

o   a parent who starts traveling a lot

o   moving away from a home, which may mean leaving behind an animal friend or an environment that allows for roaming free in nature

o   a new baby, puppy or kitten – animals can show sibling rivalry just like kids do!

o tension or even abuse within the family – animals pick up on the emotions in the household and can feel protective of one partner

o animals can be abused in a domestic violence situation – in fact, an abused animal can be an early indication of violent tendencies in a partner.

Animals are very much aware of what we are feeling and thinking. They may even be more aware than we are of something we are blind to, because of their strong sense of intuition.

For fascinating stories about animals and how much they feel and understand about human life, I love the books of Amelia Kinkade (*From the Horse's Mouth* and *The Language of Miracles*).

A stunning book about animals' feelings towards each other is Marc Bekoff's well-researched *The Emotional Lives of Animals.*

The remedy **Ignatia** is the best when an animal seems very upset or suddenly upset, perhaps with whimpering or moaning. Shirley often gives Ignatia to the shelter dogs who have just lost their owners. She says that dogs often howl when they first come to the shelter.

It's the top remedy we use when the upsetting incident just happened – someone just passed away, or the family just moved to another house.

Story Time

OJ, an appropriately-named orange cat, was one of four cats who moved into a house that already had four animals in it. OJ, like all cats, was sure he was the favorite and could not tolerate the indignity of being only one of 8 animals in the new household. Such an injustice!

To make matters worse, he had gone from a farmhouse with free range of the house and yard to being stuck inside a small house on a busy street where it was not safe for him to go outside.

OJ went on strike. He spent three months living under the owners' bed and expressing his extreme displeasure by hissing whenever he was dragged out from under. They even had to feed him under the bed because he refused to be lured out by food.

Dr. Roman recommended **Ignatia** and the owners gave him a squirt of it in his mouth (presumably squirting under the bed!). Five minutes later he went into the lviing room and rolled around in front of the other animals, making a dramatic statement in his own kitty way.

He seemed to understand that his new living situation was not what he wanted, but with the help of Ignatia, he got over it!

When the grief settles in and becomes longterm, **Nat. mur.** might be a better match. (When you find it in the health food store, the tube will give the long version of the name - Natrum muriaticum – but we call it Nat. mur. for short.)

One easy way to tell the difference – if the animal seems to be gobbling its food out of distress or frustration, it's likely to need Ignatia. (And yes, it's also for people who do emotional eating!)

Animals that seem grief-stricken or depressed longterm, while refusing to eat, are likely to need Nat. mur. They are also likely to refuse to socialize, perhaps hiding under the bed when company comes.

We typically use a 30c potency (strength) for acute situations like sudden grief or loss, so use Ignatia in a 30c.

For longterm situations, a milder form is better. Your health food store is likely to have a 6c or 12c form of Nat. mur., or you can order it online.

Story Time

Homeopath and author Miranda Castro tells of arriving at a friend's house to teach a class on cell salts (homeopathically energized minerals) and finding the friend's cat under the porch, facing into the darkest corner. The cat had been there for several days, refusing to come out or to eat.

Apparently this behavior began when a new kitten arrived and the older cat seemed to feel it had lost its special position, as everyone in the family began doting on the kitten.

When Miranda got to the cell salt **Natrum mur.**, she described its emotional aspect as silent grief, often with resentment or bitterness at a loss. The person who needs it is likely to suffer in silence rather than crying hysterically (as someone would who needed Ignatia, for example), and they may refuse to eat.

The whole class gasped, "The cat!" The cat's mum went under the porch to give it Natrum mur. (a couple of tiny tablets dissolved in the cat's mouth).

Half an hour later the cat walked through the open front door, through the living room where the class was being held, and went straight to the basket where the kitten was sleeping. She climbed into the basket, curled up around the kitten, and went to sleep!

She was absolutely fine after that. She and the kitten became fast friends. A single dose of Natrum mur. helped her to recover from the grief of losing her special place in the family's affections.

The other remedy we typically need for a pet who's upset: **Pulsatilla**, the "abandoned child" remedy.

It's not the *only* remedy for someone who feels abandoned – it depends on how they respond.

If they respond by feeling hurt and withdrawing to protect themselves against being hurt again, they are more likely to need Nat. mur. Typical Nat. mur. strategy – to protect the wounded heart by building a wall around it.

But that's likely to be the response of an older child.

If a baby or very young child feels abandoned, they are likely to cling like a little barnacle to a parent or parent figure.

They want to be really sure they are never abandoned again, so they ingratiate themselves by being very sweet and affectionate. Children will stick close to mom, climb on mommy's lap, say "I love you" and want reassurance: "Do you love me, mommy?"

Of course animals can't do that, but they can do a lot of tail-wagging and licking and pawing. And they do try to climb on your lap – even if it's a 100-pound dog trying to sit on the lap of a 100-pound adult!

They can also follow you around, staying so close to your ankles that you keep tripping over them. So you have mixed feelings – you're irritated but you know they're just trying to be affectionate – just as you might with a Pulsatilla child, who can leave you feeling a bit claustrophobic.

A lot of pets need Pulsatilla because they were taken away from their mothers too soon. Kittens, for example, are so cute at six weeks, but they really need to learn from their mothers for eight weeks. Pulsatilla 30c can help them overcome the trauma of separation.

Story Time

My first cat, Queenie, had suffered years of neglect before she came into my life. When I moved into a lovely old home in Cambridge, I found this neurotic cat who had been left behind when my landlady's daughter went away to college. The cat had suffered ten years of being harassed by the dog and ignored by my landlady, who didn't even notice when the cat was locked in the shed for a week.

By the time I moved in, my landlady was tired of feeding her and had decided to euthanize her. "You can't do that to a perfectly healthy cat!" I protested. "She's yours," was the response.

Lots of affection changed this cat's nature. She started acting like a normal cat again, except – as it turned out – when I went away for weekends. My downstairs neighbor, who was in charge of feeding her, reported, "Your cat goes crazy when you're away! Crying and crying, pawing at my door . . ."

This was a case for **Pulsatilla**! I started putting a few pellets of it in her water bowl before going away for the weekend. I tried to explain it to my neighbor, who called it the "brat cat pill."

One Sunday night as I was heading up the stairs, my neighbor stopped me. "You forgot to give her the brat cat pill, didn't you?"

She was right. How can you explain this by the placebo effect? My neighbor could tell the remedy's action just by observing the cat!

Herbs and Flower Essences for Emotional Healing

Rescue Remedy is great for an animal that is upset. It's a blend of five flower essences – remedies made with water infused with flower petals.

Might sound too dilute to make a difference, but just try it. Many people have found that **Rescue Remedy** helps animals with any emotional trauma — not just grief, but also anxiety, for example when riding in the car, or when the family is packing suitcases for traveling, or when the animal is going to the vet.

(By the way, how on earth do animals know they are going to the vet? Did you ever wonder about that?)

How to give Rescue Remedy

You can squirt it with a syringe into the mouth, but a spray bottle is easier. Ideally use an opaque bottle like from a hairdresser's supply store. You'll use these a lot, and you need a different one for each remedy, so you might want to get a dozen while you're there. They need to be clean and never used for anything before.

For a 12 oz. bottle use 2 full droppers of Rescue Remedy, 1/2 tsp of alcohol as a preservative, then fill with spring water. Succuss (give it hard whack) 30 times.

Options for a preservative: Peach brandy has a special affinity for flower essences. (A clear alcohol such as vodka is used for homeopathic remedies). Or if you want to avoid alcohol, use vegetable glycerine, available in drugstores. Use a tablespoonful, as it's not as good a preservative as alcohol, and refrigerate the mixture if you want to keep it longterm.

Mist Rescue Remedy onto the animal – this works especially well with large animals like horses. You can mist a whole horse this way!

Or (especially with cats, who hate sprays!) mist it onto your hands and rub the head and ears. Doesn't matter if it doesn't reach the skin – it works energetically. You can do the same thing with **lavender and frankincense essential oils**. Make up a separate spray bottle for each one, putting a few drops of essential oil into the bottle to create an aerosol dispersion. Essential oils don't need a preservative – just discard if you see sediment at the bottom.

This can be used to **calm a barking dog!**

At Save A Dog, they make a spray bottle of lavender and chamomile and spray it around the kennel to calm the dogs down. If a dog is very stressed and barking, they just lightly spray it around that dog's kennel and it seems to quiet the dog down. Shirley makes a 6 oz. bottle, adding mostly distilled water and then a couple of drops of the **lavender/chamomile** scent, available in natural food stores.

When they take in new dogs into the shelter, if they are especially frightened, we give them homeopathic **Aconite.** It not only helps with the fear, but it helps curtail the break-down of the immune system that usually happens when an animal is frightened.

For cats, **catnip** can be either really distracting or extra stimulating when they are upset! Most cats love it (a few don't react at all). Try putting fresh or dried catnip in the cat carrier to keep your cat happy while traveling. For outdoor cats, try planting cat mint in the garden – mine revel in it.

Calming an overly aggressive dog

Over-aggression in dogs may be related to too many rabies vaccines, as suggested by Dr. Don Hamilton in his highly recommended book *Homeopathic Medicine for Cats and Dogs*. Please consider keeping rabies vaccines to the minimum going forward, especially for aggressive dogs. A homeopathic vet can eliminate the side effects of the rabies vaccine with professional homeopathic care.

Another factor to consider: the lack of essential fatty acids. The connection is clear in humans; in one study, prisoners given a daily essential fatty acid supplement had a significant reduction in violent, aggressive behavior.

Essential fatty acids are destroyed when food is heated as part of processing or canning. And feeding raw foods is no guarantee, because conventional meat has the wrong balance of essential fatty acids. Only organic, grass-fed and grass-finished meat will have the beneficial ratio. So a good solution is to supplement, for example with salmon oil.

Another solution: "Dog Appeasing Pheromones", or D.A.P. can relax dogs – easily available online, and now availble in collar form so the dog is calmed constantly.

Some behavioral approaches: a good trainer can help (see resources for finding a trainer on page 100). And sometimes the dogs just need more exercise outdoors. Dogs in nature would be hunting their own food, getting lots of exercise. If they are fed and kept cooped up inside, they get bored and restless and can behave aggressively.

For some dogs, another dog to play with will help. But of course, this won't work if the aggressive dog keeps attacking the other dog! So you need to know your dog and his needs.

Calming a dying animal

Arsenicum will relax your pet, reduce its anxiety and make this passage easier. Even better, alternate it with **Rescue Remedy:**

- o Make a 4 ounce (half cup) solution of each one separately.

- o A few pellets of Arsenicum 6c or 30c in a cup of water

- o 4 or 5 drops of Rescue Remedy in another cup

- o Every two minutes give one of them, alternately.

You also need to give your pet permission to go. Its human family will need Ignatia when losing a beloved companion. Write down what your pet meant to you, what you learned from it, how much love you shared with it, your favorite memories.

If your pet is in extreme pain, consider euthanasia from a vet. But an animal supported with healthy food and a healthy lifestyle is likely to live long then fade away naturally, without pain. Allowing them to do that in their own time, in their own home, is a cherished time for the family and eases the pain of parting.

Sources of flower essences for animals

Green Hope Farms is a wonderful source of flower essences for animals. Many people like their **Animal Rescue,** which is like Rescue Remedy made especially for animals. www.greenhopeessences.com

By the way, we also use their **Flea Free** a lot!

Another great source: **Spirit Essence** flower essences for animals, made by a vet and an animal behaviorist. www.spiritessence.com.

If you read through their products, you will be amazed at all the different emotional and behavioral problems in animals that can be addressed by flower essences.

This idea may sound hokey (like, how can these thigns possibly work?) but these companies have an excellent reputation in the holistic veterinary community. Their products are definitely worth a try if you're having a behavior problem with your pet. Like many things recommended in this book, they are harmless and relatively inexpensive, so why not try the natural route first?

And if you'd like to try Rescue Remedy for yourself or a stressed family member, you can find it in any natural food store, with more information about it at www.nelsonsnaturalworld.com.

Rescue Tales from Save A Dog

Shirley generously provides care for people who cannot afford vet services, like a woman who had adopted a feral cat at 8 weeks (something Shirley would never recommend, but the woman loved the cat). The cat was really wild – it bit the woman on the arm every day, so her arms were all bloodied.

The woman had cancer and had no money so Shirley offered a simple solution. She just asked whether the cat's pupils dilated before it attacked. The answer was yes, so Shirley was pretty sure the cat would benefit from homeopathic Belladonna. (There are a number of remedies for aggression and violent rage in homeopathy, and the dilated pupils narrowed down the choice to Belladonna.)

The woman gave a single dose of **Belladonna 30c** and immediately the cat stopped biting her!

As is typical for these remedies, though, the effect wore off over time, and the remedy had to be repeated in a higher dose (200c, the next highest potency available). Even that wore off, and the cat needed the next potency: 1M, or 1000c. When last heard from it was still working and the cat and her 'mother' were living together peacefully.

Shirley says the most touching part of this story is the woman's report that after a few doses of Belladonna, "one morning, for the first time, I woke up with the cat snuggling next to me." Anyone who has tried to tame a feral cat can tell you how amazing that is!

Your Pet's Personality

The major homeopathic remedies are not only medicines for specific conditions – they are also personality types!

Here are some of the most common types. (We call them **constitutional types** in homeopathy.) Your pet might not fit any of these descriptions, but if she does, you're lucky because right away you know the best remedy to give her. The constitutional remedy can be given seasonally to keep your pet healthy, and it's also likely to be a good remedy for her when she gets sick.

You might even recognize yourself or your children in these descriptions! They have been more fully described for people, and you can read about several dozen of these types in Catherine Coulter's delightful *Nature and Human Personality.* If you don't recognize your pet's personality here, you'll probably find it in Catherine Coulter's book. (She's a homeopath, not the author of the supermarket romance novels.)

If you are sure of your pet's constitutional type, you can try using it when they're sick, and also once a season as a general strengthener, in a 200c potency.

Phosphorus – Star of the Show

Does your dog love to be the center of attention? Is she friendly and gregarious? Does she go up to greet strangers and appear to bask in the limelight of their attention? Did she take to learning tricks easily and does she love to perform? Your dog might be a Phosphorus type!

Dr. Roman says she can tell right away when a Phosphorus dog comes to the office. The dog is bubbly and friendly and can't wait to meet the vet.

Another way she can tell the dog's constitution is to ask the owner how the dog behaves at a party. A Phosphorus wants to be right in the middle of things, greeting everyone and thriving on the attention. This is also the dog that loves to show off a little bow in her fur!

Each of these types has its weak points, though. Phosphorus types can be more prone to coughs and to bleeding, and these are the dogs who hide under the bed during a thunderstorm. Phosphorus as a remedy (30c potency) is the first remedy to try for all these problems in a Phosphorus-type dog. (It's the first remedy for bleeding and for fear of thunderstorms for *any* dog. Coughs are tricky, though – Phosphorus is one of *many* cough remedies.)

Calc. carb. – the Chow Hound

While Phosphorus animals tend to have a more slender, willowy build, the Calc. carb. type is likely to be sturdy, robust or stout. "Big boned" is the euphemism that Calc carb women use for themselves!

Calc. carbs are real foodies, always focused on where the next meal is coming from. At a party, they would contentedly accept a pat on the head, but their main focus is watching for someone to drop food on the floor. Fair game for a Calc. carb!

My beloved pure white cat Princess was a Calc. carb. – she had an insatiable appetite and a bit of a melon-belly. She threw up all the time because she ate too much. I used to tell her, "Sweetie, your palace name is Princess Bulimia and your street name is Barf Girl!"

They are also homebodies with a placid temperament. They wouldn't be in the owner's lap, like a Pulsatilla dog, but they would like to be close by. Having their parent in sight leaves them content and relaxed. They get anxious when their parent starts to disappear … so they will follow them around, even into the bathroom.

They are strong but a little lethargic – it can be hard to get them to move. This type would be a bit of a couch potato!

One weak area for them is bones and joints. They may be more likely to need the joint supplement recommended on page 14 to prevent sprains and strains, which they are extra-susceptible to. They can also have growth plate issues with their bones.

Another problem area is moist ear issues, which are likely to respond to the remedy Calc. carb.

Sulphur — Smart and Strong

These animals like to watch what's going on and analyze everything! They are the ones that the owner will describe as "a really smart dog." They are also more athletic than the others and more apt to enjoy a good hard game of frisbee.

They seem to have an inner strength, too – they are confident and secure in themselves. At a party they might have their own favorites among the guests but would not waste their time on others.

They seem to have an attitude towards life like, "Just deal with it." And if you could hear them talking to the little Pulsatillas in the next section, they would probably be saying, "Just grow up and get over it."

A tip-off for Sulphurs: they hate baths and being groomed. They can't stand being fussed over. What a waste of time! They have places to go and things to do. This tends to be a male type. Does it remind you of any guys you might know?

They also tend to run hotter than other dogs. One way you can tell is that they are more likely to sleep in the shade than in the sun.

The weak point for this type is the skin. They are the most likely to have skin issues. (In a way, this represents their strength. Holistic healers believe in healing from the inside out. If the animal's healing energy can push a problem to the very surface, that's much better than creating a more serious disease deeper inside.)

So Sulphur is often the first remedy to try in skin conditions. You have to be careful, though, because in homeopathy, too much of a remedy can boomerang and make things worse. You don't want to make a skin condition worse, especially if it's itchy!

So you can try Sulphur 6c (low potency) for *any* pet with a skin condition, and if your pet has a Sulphur constitution it is *especially* likely to work.

Pulsatilla — the Baby of the Family

Pulsatilla types are sweet and charming – and they use their charms to manipulate you! They are extremely affectionate and love to nuzzle and cuddle. They love to sit on mommy's lap. They will follow you around like a Calc. carb.

The difference is that Calc. carb. is content as long as you are somewhere nearby, but a Pulsatilla wants to be touching you. This is the dog that sits next to you on the sofa and keeps proffering a paw, or the cat that purrs and purrs and burrows her head into you. (All these types apply to dogs, cats, actually all animals – and people!)

They are clingy, dependent, and needy, and in dogs this comes out as whining, whining, whining until they get what they want. They can drive you a little nuts! Since these types crave fresh air and gentle exercise, what they want is likely to be a walk or at least an open window.

Their weak point is the digestive system, and they might be likely to throw up. You can't identify the type just based on barfing tendencies, though. A Sulphur dog might throw up because he just ate garbage (a Sulphur specialty), and a Calc. carb. might throw up because she just ate too much (like my Princess!)

Arsenicum — Nervous Neat Freaks

This is the fastidious, anxious type. Cats are likely to be an Arsenicum type. In humans, Arsenicums are anxious about health, money, having a roof over their heads or maybe becoming homeless, just about anything to do with their needs. Their anxiety about health leads them to be extreme neat freaks. They see germs everywhere. Purell was made for these people.

So you can imagine why we often see cats as Arsenicums. All cats groom themselves, though, and not all cats have this nervous personality. My black-and-white tomcat Sammy grooms himself just like any other cat and he is definitely not an Arsenicum — he is a smart and athletic Sulphur. Plus he grooms himself with a lick and a promise, and he doesn't care. His sister Misty tries to clean the spots he missed and he bats her away with his big paws. Typical Sulphur — lazy and messy!

But if you have a pet that seems nervous and tense, with a tendency to groom constantly, this might be an Arsenicum type. Arsenicum is a great remedy for so many things — diarrhea, food poisoning, runny noses — give it a try when a pet of this type is sick.

Rescue Tales from Save A Dog

This is a story that shows how, in homeopathy, each condition can have multiple remedies that might cure it, and each remedy can work for different conditions.

Save A Dog had a little chihuahua mix called Superman because he was always jumping over things and onto things, like a little jumping bean. He would jump onto his crate and sleep on top, or even jump onto a shelf!

He had kennel cough which did not respond to the usual remedies like Aconite, Spongia, Hepar sulph or Drosera. Nothing was working.

Then Shirley realized that **Arsenicum**, although not usually used as a cough remedy, matched his overall demeanor. People who are sick and need Arsenicum are typically very restless, and that's exactly what Superman was like: he just could not stay still.

She gave him Arsenicum 1M (a high dose) and the cough was gone in two days.

It was so dramatic, the staff kept asking, "What happened?"

Arsenicum is usually used for food poisoning with vomiting and/or watery diarrhea; feline asthma with wheezing; and preventively when exposed to another animal that's sick.

Also for anxiety and restlessness, and especially for all these physical conditions when your pet is anxious and restless.

Pets and Their People —
Same Personality Type?

So here's the funny thing. A lot of Arsenicum-type pets have Arsenicum-type owners! This is the person endlessly worried about her health and/or her pet's health. If one lab test comes back normal, it must be wrong so she has to get another one, and if the first doctor can't diagnose the problem, she will keep going from one practitioner to another – holistic as well as conventional – until she has accumulated an inch-thick medical record and a bag full of drugs and supplements.

Vets often see this connection between the personality type of pets and their owners! In fact, they may have the same diagnosis (hypothyroidism, diabetes, etc.) and need the same homeopathic remedy.

I can vouch for this because Margo sometimes refers an owner to me, and we often find that she is giving the pet the same remedy that I am giving to the owner!

Same Diseases?

Margo says that holistic vets have all noticed this phenomenon and have discussed it many times at conferences. They believe that an energetic communication or energetic field is shared between the pet and its owner.

There can also be a practical explanation: pets and their caretakers share the same water, live in the same environment, and are exposed to the same toxins.

I can say from my days as a health food store owner that many people embark on a holistic lifestyle because they tried it first for their pets. Margo feels that pets can bring us awareness of how well holistic treatment works and they inspire us to take better care of ourselves.

Coincidence or — Unconditional Love?

In fact, many holistic vets believe that pets who are ill with serious diseases such as cancer are actually taking the disease on behalf of the owner. They have accepted the disease that the owner was destined to get and they are willing to die if necessary to save the owner. Dogs are especially likely to do this, vets feel, because dogs embody unconditional love.

You may not believe this unless you experience it for yourself. We are mentioning it so that if it happens to you and your pet, you will be aware of it and give your pet so much love and gratitude for the sacrifice she is making.

A wonderful book about the relationship between humans and their pets is *Kindred Spirits* by Dr. Allen Schoen.

Raw! Raw! Raw!

Dogs and cats did not evolve in the wild by opening cans of food. Surprise!

Now, I know what you're thinking. (Scary, isn't it? I know what you're thinking!) You're saying, okay, they also didn't evolve by opening bottles of vitamins!

Even if we given them fresh organic raw ground turkey meat from Whole Foods (and yes, this is what my spoiled little darlings get), it doesn't have the range of nutrients they would get in the wild.

Carnivores in the wild crunch on bones, feathers and skin. They eat organs like heart, liver and kidneys, each of which has special nutrients. And the essential fatty acid content of wild game is much more beneficial than what's in modern commercially-raised meat.

More importantly, they're eating the stomach contents of their prey – getting partially digested seeds and grasses. So they're getting greens, digestive enzymes, and gut bacteria (probiotics).

So unless we want to go out and catch mice and lizards and birds for our little darlings, we need to find a way to reproduce their traditional food, doing the best we can with raw foods and supplements.

Okay, I know what you're thinking – *It's too expensive!* You think you can't afford it. But guess what – it's either pay for good quality food now (and enjoy healthy, happy, flea-free pets with beautiful glossy coats) OR wait until they get some major disease and THEN pay thousands of dollars for drugs and/or surgery.

OR you may even have to have your pet put to sleep because it's so sick.

So you pay now or pay later. If you pay now, you get to enjoy your pets with a milder, gentler temperament.

Still not convinced about raw, fresh, natural food? Do a little reading about what's in commercial pet food. *Hint:* it's gross. It includes ground up roadkill and tumors from diseased animals (which became people food after the tumors were cut out!). Don't believe us? Check it out for yourself, for example on www.truthaboutpetfood.com.

Fallacies about raw food

Food poisoning: Opponents of raw foods (who often coincidentally work for, or sell, commercial pet food) say there's a problem with salmonella or E.coli – but vets like Dr. Roman who recommend a raw food diet never see this type of food poisoning as a result. Margo says not a single case in 25 years of a recommending raw foods! Pets that eat raw have fewer parasites because their guts are stronger.

It's true that you have to be careful handling raw meat for your pets – just as you would for your family. Don't let the juices get on vegetables to be eaten raw, or on dishes in the sink. Be especially careful if you are immune-compromised yourself.

Here's another myth: animals will **crack their teeth** on the bones, or **swallow a splintered bone.** Actually, animals that chew on raw bones have healthier teeth! And you'll save on vet bills for teeth cleaning.

Dr. Roman reports that she's never had an animal get a raw bone stuck in its throat. Cooked bones, yes, but never raw.

Raw chicken bones are more rubbery than cooked ones, which *could* splinter. Chickens are slaughtered at 10-12 weeks, before their bones are fully hardened - that's why it's safe.

Also if you're cooking them in a stew, cooking them for a long time until theyre mushy, that's also safe. Bones from a grilled chicken could definitely splinter and cause problems.

More advantages of chewing raw bones

Puppies need to chew! It helps massage the gums, bring out the adult teeth, and shed the baby teeth. If you don't give them bones, they'll find something else – like your favorite shoe or sofa.

Chewing raw bones also gives them the calcium and other minerals to build their bones in the proper ratio.

Here's the most amazing one: a puppy with a misaligned jaw (say, the canine teeth hitting the palate) would normally need surgery to correct it (and remember how expensive vet surgery is, not to mention traumatic for the pet).

BUT if you catch the situation early, let them chew on raw bones, and give them the remedy **Calc. carb**. 1M, their jaws may align by themselves! (1M refers to a high potency or very strong version of the remedy, available online but not in stores.)

Switching your pet to a raw foods diet

Shirley advises people to put their dogs on probiotics (see page 111) for a couple of weeks before switching to raw by introducing it a 1/4 teaspoon at a time, mixed into their food.

Another option is to fast the dog for 24-48 hours, but she says most owners are not willing to do that. If the dog is already not eating because of problems with the commercially prepared diet, then they can switch right away. However, if the dog is in poor health, you can't switch to raw foods too quickly because their intestines are weakened from commercial dog food.

She starts them with a recipe from Dr. Richard Pitcairn's *Complete Guide to Naural Health for Dogs & Cats.* You definitely need this book because it's full of other recipes (including the all-important **Healthy Powder**!) and nutritional information.

Doggie Oats

2 cups raw rolled oats (or 4 cups cooked oatmeal)

½ pound (1 cup) raw ground or chopped turkey

2 tablespoons Healthy Powder

1 tablespoon vegetable oil

¼ cup cooked vegetables (or less if raw and grated)

1,500 mg calcium or ¾ tsp eggshell powder

2,500 - 5,000 IU Vitamin A (optional if using carrots)

100 IU Vitamin E

1 small clove Garlic, crushed or minced (optional)

5 milligrams Iron (optional)

Rescue Tales from Save A Dog

Shirley says it's easier to switch young dogs to raw foods. She had a five-month-old Labradoodle with a torn cruciate ligament. She fed it ground duck (a cooling, anti-inflammatory food in Traditional Chinese Medicine) and mixed in

- o   cooked sweet potato

- o   green beans

- o   essential fatty acid oil

- o   probiotics

- o   **TurmericForce** by New Chapter Vitamins*

She says "I had a new dog in a month!"

*New Chapter Vitamins are excellent food-based vitamins for people. TurmericForce is an anti-inflammatory, good for people as well as pets.

Quick Tip: Make It Work for You and Your Pet

Here's an example of how you might adapt the recipes to what works for you. I've developed a routine based on what my cats like PLUS what's quick and easy for me. This takes about 10 minutes once a week!

Note that this is not the ideal raw foods diet. Dr. Karen Becker's book *Real Food for Healthy Dogs and Cats* teaches the best way to do it – but after 40 years as a vegetarian, I just can't grind raw meat in a meatgrinder. Handling ground raw food from Whole Foods is the best I can do.

So I mix organic ground turkey meat with some canned salmon with the bones, so the kitty-darlings get some bones to chew on, then add

- o a probiotic-digestive enzyme mix
- o some powdered spirulina or blue-green algae for the chlorophyll
- o powdered bone meal

I'm not giving you amounts because I've had to experiment to see how much I can add of each before they turn up their little pink noses at the mixture. Each cat will be different.

I mix in big batches and freeze it in deli containers like hummus containers – each one is enough for one day for two cats, so it's always fresh.

As I'm serving it, I add a squirt of salmon oil for the essential fatty acids, from a bottle I keep in the refrigerator.

Once a week or so, they each get an egg from a cage-free chicken.

For variety, they have a limited tolerance for canned sardines – I always add extra enzymes and probiotics when using canned food.

Raw fish would be healthier but I just can't tolerate the smell.

Dr. Roman wants me to add that raw fish is fine for pets EXCEPT salmon from the Northwest, as it has liver flukes which can poison dogs.

I also give them raw chicken bones to chew on, once a week or so. That way their teeth get cleaned naturally, like they would in the wild. (Which is good because I draw the line at brushing their teeth for them!)

Healthy Gums: And by the way, you should pull back their cheeks to check their gums once in a while.
A red line around the base of their teeth indicates a gum infection, which could mean trouble down the road. Give a dose of **Sulphur 30c** each time you see that warning sign.

Gum infections can lead to tooth infections, which can affect the whole body because each tooth is on one of the meridians (energetic pathways) leading to a particular organ in the body.

Also an infected tooth can be painful and prevent your pet from chewing his food well.

So lots of good reasons to get your pet chomping on some raw bones!

A great source of frozen raw foods: hare-today.com.

Story Time

I take my cats to Dr. Margo Roman when they're sick, but she's an hour away, so for routine things like a rabies shot I take them to a local vet.

There was a lot of eye-rolling and a bit of sermonizing on a recent visit when I shared my beliefs about raw foods and minimal vaccinations. Plus I refused the standard heartworm and flea medications urged on me by the vet.

When it was time to go I opened the cat carrier and Sammy and Misty paraded in of their own volition, tails held high.

The vet and vet tech looked at each other in disbelief. Have you ever tried to get a cat into a cat carrier? It's like trying to strap a resistant, back-arching toddler into a car seat. It can take two strong adults per cat to wrestle it into a cat carrier.

"It's because I feed them raw foods with essential fatty acids," I said, trying not to sound too smug about my kitties' docile dispositions!

Story Time

The oldest dog I ever saw– *by Dr. Margo Roman*

In 1978 I was doing an internship at Angell Memorial Hospital, one of the most prestigious animal hospitals in the world. So I felt entitled to question the owner of a 21-year-old Alaskan Eskimo with a mammary tumor the size of a grapefruit hanging from her breast.

First I asked him what dog food he fed her.

"I'm homeless," he replied. "I can't afford to buy dog food. She eats what I eat. Whatever I can pick up from the shelter or a restaurant, I share with her – a piece of meat, vegetables, salad or stew."

I lectured him about how he had to buy dog food because it's balanced, and how can you balance the diet if you're just giving table scraps?

Next I asked him about her vaccination status. "I've never taken her to the vet, so she's never had a vaccination since she was a puppy," he replied. "I can't even afford to go to the doctor for myself."

I lectured him about distemper, parvo and all the other diseases she could get without the protection of vaccinations. "She's never been sick," he replied.

Next I lectured him about not having her spayed. We learned in veterinary school that spaying helps to prevent cancer, and mammary cancer in particular. Spaying could have saved her from dying of cancer. "She's had the tumor for seven years," was the response.

I discounted him as an unintelligent and unsophisticated dog owner who had damaged his dog by not vaccinating, not spaying, not feeding commercial food – but his dog was 21 with all its teeth and looking like a healthy 7-year-old dog!

So that was a big learning experience for me.

Story Time

The oldest cat I ever saw – *by Dr. Margo Roman*

In 1976 I was doing an externship at a prestigious location – the Animal Medical Center in New York. A woman brought in a 25-year-old male Siamese who was friendly, in great health, with all its teeth. I asked her what cat food she fed him.

"I never give cat food. I prepare fresh meat and fresh food for him."

Feeling at the top of my game, I lectured her about feeding cat food because it's properly balanced.

"But you don't know what's in it!" she replied. "You know what you feed your animal when you make it yourself."

Next I asked about the cat's vaccination status.

"I don't vaccinate my cat," she replied. "I don't think I need to put all those extra vaccines into my cat."

Well, I discounted her as an arrogant know-it-all who thought she knew more than a professional vet.

Lo and behold, ten years later I reflected on the oldest dog and the oldest cat I ever saw, taken care of by people who did not follow anything we were taught in vet school.

So who was the arrogant know-it-all after all?

I still to this day have not seen elderly animals as healthy and thriving as those two.

Tummy Troubles

Dogs eat garbage. It's what they do.

Cats swallow hairballs. It's what they do.

Both throw up. What can you do?

We have two top remedies for **vomiting**:

Nux vomica (sounds like it's for vomiting, doesn't it?) and **Arsenicum** (sounds like a poison, doesn't it? It's for food poisoning!)
They both can be used for any problem with the digestive system.

Nux vomica is used especially when your pet is irritable and grumpy, even aggressive when touched.
It covers dry heaves and retching better than Arsenicum does.

Arsenicum is used when your pet is anxious and restless. It covers watery diarrhea better than Nux does.

Honestly, it can be hard to tell the difference.

Try one for several doses, in a 30c potency and if no change, try the other. You can also make them stronger by putting them in water and succussing (whacking) the bottle.

Doggy diarrhea - yuck!

The same two remedies are used for diarrhea:

Nux vomica when there is vomiting

Arsenicum when the diarrhea is watery. Shirley says that for her rescue dogs, she uses Arsenicum "because they are coming off bad food from their previous place."

Let's add one more great diarrhea remedy:

Podophyllum, for painless, watery, gushing diarrhea. We call it "fire hydrant diarrhea." Got the picture?

Possible Poisoning

If your pet swallowed something toxic such as a medication, household chemical, certain houseplants, or chocolate (really toxic for dogs!), call Animal Poison Control. Sometimes they can tell you what to do at home so you don't have to go to the animal hospital.

Animal Poison Control 24-Hour Hotline

Before you call, note the time your pet was exposed to the toxin, the type of product ingested, the manufacturer's name and any ingredients you can find listed on the packaging. Expect to pay a $65 fee for this service.

ASPCA Animal Poison Control Center   1.888.426.4435

And this is a good moment to say – please throw away all conventional household cleaning supplies, all of which contain toxic chemicals, and replace them with environmentally friendly ones – which are also safer for you and your pets. Otherwise they will get toxic chemicals on their paws and lick their paws.

You would do this for a toddler in the house – please do it for your pets.

Environmental Working Group, www.ewg.org, is an excellent resource for learning about toxic chemicals you don't want in the house.

Debra Dadd's books such as *Home Safe Home* and *Really Green* are great resources for safe substitutes. Natural cleansers are so effective (and so cheap!) there's no longer any reason to use commercial ones.

Inducing vomiting

You may need to induce vomiting with hydrogen peroxide (see instructions below), or give activated charcoal. (Induce vomiting UNLESS it's a substance like bleach which can be harmful on the way back up, in which case give activated charcoal to neutralize it in the digestive system.) It's wise to keep both on hand. You'll want the activated charcoal in powder form (food grade) rather than capsules, and you can get it online.

How to use hydrogen peroxide

For a small dog (under 50 lbs.) give a teaspoon.
For larger dogs, give a tablespoon into the mouth
It starts to foam in the back of the throat, they gag and throw up.

You can do that three times 10 minutes apart.

If you can't get them to vomit and it might be toxic, you need to get them to an emergency vet.

If they do vomit, make sure they don't scarf up the vomit stuff! Dogs will do this with chocolate that they just threw up. You went to get something to wipe it up . . . they helped you out by using their tongue . . .

How to Give Activated Charcoal

Give about 1 gram per pound of your pet's weight, mix with water, and administer with a syringe. Just don't give it if your pet swallowed a caustic substance (containing lye). Administer while waiting to reach Animal Poison Control or the vet, especially if your dog has eaten chocolate.

Abdominal Obstructions

If your pet keeps vomiting even when there is nothing more in its stomach, and you've given the remedies to no avail, it may have swallowed something which is blocking its digestive tract. Try giving vaseline (petroleum jelly) to help the obstruction slip through.

o   For a medium size dog: a heaping tablespoonful

o   For a larger dog like a Lab, 1/4 cup

o   If they won't eat it, put it between 2 pieces of bread

o   Repeat in an hour

The most important concern in this situation is keeping your pet hydrated. If the intestinal tract becomes dehydrated, it clamps down on the objects and becomes bruised and then the object cannot pass.

But if you can keep your pet hydrated and lubricated with vaseline, they can pass surprising objects! Dr. Margo says you can't imagine what she has seen dogs pass using vaseline, like a 2'x5' towel and a 2'x8' piece of fabric!

But if the vaseline doesn't work, it can be a life-threatening problem. If you can reach your holistic vet, this blockage can often be resolved by using ozone therapy, homeopathic remedies (**Nux vomica** and **Calendula**) and acupuncture. If not, go to your nearest animal hospital where surgery will probably be required.

This can even happen when cats swallow string and the intestines become bruised. String is surprisingly dangerous (and tempting) for cats, so try to keep strings, thread, yarn, and dental floss away from them.

Hairballs are another source of intestinal blockage in cats. For ways to prevent hairballs, see page 58.

Remedies for Abdominal Obstructions

Dr. Patricia Jordan – one of our holistic vet friends – says **Phosphorus** can work when the obstruction is in the stomach and **Calendula** when it's further down. Not sure where it is? Try both in alternation.

Do it on the way to the emergency animal hospital, though. We can't guarantee it will work. But it's harmless and worth a shot and may spare your pet (and you!) from unnecessary surgery.

Story Time

Dr. Margo Roman had a client whose most precious possession was a gorgeous leather beaded vest he had worn to Woodstock. (She saw the same thing in a photo at the Rock 'n Roll Hall of Fame – apparently it was quite the thing to wear back then!)

Unfortunately his Lab ate the whole thing – beads and all! She told him to give the dog a vaseline sandwich with 1/4 cup of vaseline smeared between two pieces of white bread, and then to repeat it in an hour.

He did, and the dog passed the whole thing – all the beads and scraps of leather – but he was never able to reconstruct the vest.

Preventing Hairballs in Cats

The best method is the simplest – when cats are shedding, brush them with a wire brush. Many cats LOVE this, I mean they go into ECSTASY when they are brushed. (You can buy a special grooming brush, but my cats are fine with an inexpensive hairbrush from the drugstore, the kind with thin stiff bristles.) The more hairs you can remove, the less will go down your kitty's throat.

They *will* swallow some hair, though, and when it gets clumped up in their digestive system, it can block thngs up.

Dr. Roman's top tip for preventing this, surprisingly, is to have them chew on **raw chicken necks**. The stringiness of the raw chicken necks sort of flosses their teeth, she says.Plus the small bones grab onto the hair balls and break them up.

A small pat of butter or a natural vegetable-oil-based product would be another way to break up the hairballs and help them pass.

Vaseline or petroleum-based products are *not* recommended because using vaseline longterm is not healthy. (One dose in an emergency situation – the "vaseline sandwich" – is okay.)

Ear Problems — Listen Up!

Ear problems are one of the top reasons for a trip to the vet – but you can often treat them at home. Most vets use antibiotics when they see an ear discharge, but most of the time the drugs are unnecessary.

Start with good ear hygiene. When there is wax buildup, clean the ears with cotton balls – first, one steeped in warm **green tea** to loosen the wax, then several dry cotton balls to wipe it out. (To steep green tea, pour 1/3 cup of boiling water over a green teabag and let it sit until it has cooled off.)

Pour a tablespoon into the ear, hold the ear closed, and massage the ear well, loosening the wax with the warm green tea. Then thrust the cotton ball into the ear canal and wipe it in a circle quite vigorously to get all the ear wax off. Repeat the green tea, then cotton ball until you can't get any more out. Finish with a dry cotton ball.

A dog has a deep, L-shaped ear canal so you're unlikely to reach the ear drum with a Q tip. As long as you can see the tip inside the ear, you're safe.

If your pet continues to scratch her ear or dig a paw deep into her ear, you want to treat her – for her own comfort, and to prevent her from damaging the inside of her ear with a claw.

The problem might be **food allergies** – a great reason to switch to raw whole foods, if you haven't yet. Ear problems, like skin problems, reflect the health of the whole system. Dr. Roman calls the ears the "dumping ground" for toxins from the whole body.

If switching to raw foods doesn't help, try a really simple, **allergen-free diet:** switch to a protein source your pet has never had before (typically venison or rabbit - try www.haretoday.com for frozen rabbit). Use with fresh vegetables and greens and healthy fiber.

Because ear problems represent inflammation systemically in the body, you want to use a cooling food like duck, fish or rabbit to reduce the heat in the body. Giving it raw also has a cooling effect.

You may have to try different protein sources. Just as people with food allergies, animals with food allergies tend to become sensitized to foods they have had a lot. So they may be allergic to the common protein sources: chicken, turkey, beef and lamb.

You may also have to change the vegetables and grain. Some animals can't tolerate gluten, which means you have to avoid wheat. Brown rice, millet and quinoa ("KEEN-wah") are the least allergenic grains for animals. (They are all available in natural food stores along with cooking directions.) Some animals can tolerate oats, which have some gluten but are lower in gluten than wheat. In general, dogs do not do well on corn.

Some animals are allergic to animal protein in general, so to clear up their ear problems you would have to give them vegetable sources of protein.

If changing the diet doesn't help, the problem could be **ear mites.** A dark black discharge, like burnt lasagna, typically means ear mites, but to be sure look under a magnifying glass for little wigglies moving around!

The simplest thing is to use a miticide (pesticide that kills mites) – otherwise you have to commit to doing the following protocol every three days for a while. Also this natural approach won't work if there are other animals in the house because they'll just keep passing the mites back and forth. Lots of ear-scratching!

If you want to go all natural and avoid using the miticide, you can use **mineral oil** (or **olive oil,** which will take longer). Put the oil in the ears and wipe out the debris really well, then wash the ears really well, then wash the cat really well (and at this point you're probably ready to give up and try the miticide) . . . then you need to leave oil in the ears to suffocate the mites.

Also put natural flea powder on the animal's head, such as **Buck Moutain Parasite Dust** (a neem-based flea and tick repellent). Or you can use a **chrysanthemum-based** product such as the one from PetGuard (although it says it's not for cats). Remember the mites can stay on the fur and then jump onto the furniture, only to return later, so you need to kill them with natural flea powder.

Another option – wash your cat with an all-natural shampoo such as **Pop's Organic Pet Shampoo** or **Dr. Bronner's Castile Soap**. Wash around the ears, clean the ears well, then dry them off.

Ear problems can also be a result of overvaccination, which you can treat with **Thuja** 30c, changing to a healthy diet and adding nutrients like essential fatty acids and antioxidants, and often that's enough to clear up an ear problem.

Whew! that means you don't have to wrestle your cat into a bathtub every three days! (My hot tip for getting a cat to cooperate with a bath: make sure the water is warm. That's made a huge difference in cooperation levels with my cats, and no more gouged arms for me!)

Remedies for ear infections

If there's a discharge from the ears but no mites, here are the top homeopathic remedies to try:

Sulphur if the discharge is dark or black

Calc. carb. if the animal is overweight and looks like a Calc. carb. (see "Calc. carb. – the Chow Hound," page 34)

Mercurius if the discharge is greenish and the skin inside the ear looks red and raw

Pulsatilla if the discharge is creamy;
if it changes back and forth from one ear to the other
or if the animal is whiny like a Pulsatilla.
(see "Pulsatilla – the Baby of the Family," page 36)

Rescue Tales from Save A Dog

Shirley Moore reports a number of successes with treating ear infections with **Pulsatilla**.

"Once I treated a little Chinese Crested puppy who had a raging ear infection and pus coming out of both ears. We gave her a dose of Pulsatilla and the next day her ears were all cleared up and dried out.

"We have since treated many dogs with these type of ear problems with Pulsatilla, to the amazement of the staff.

"It's hard to be an unbeliever when you see the change right before your eyes!"

Chronic ear and skin problems

Chronic ear problems cannot be resolved with antibiotics or other medications. They just suppress the problem – they sweep it under the rug for a while, and the ear problem will keep coming back.

Skin problems are the same way – they represent a deeper disorder. Any chronic problem is best treated by an integrative vet, but there are a couple of things you can try for skin problems:

o **Sulphur 6c**, one dose

o **Graphites 6c** if there is a yellowish wet discharge that may dry and form a crust.

Make sure to get the mild 6c potency. The 30c potency most easily found in natural food stores is too strong for chronic skin problems and may make the condition temporarily worse – and your animal will be miserable.

If you're lucky the Sulphur or Graphites 6c will work. Otherwise, be sure to take your pet to an integrative vet, because skin problems are a surface symptom indicating that things are really going wrong inside. Your pet not only needs holistic modalities for the skin problem, but more importantly for the deeper problems showing up on the skin.

It's actually lucky your pet is getting skin problems — otherwise you wouldn't know about the deeper issues until it's too late!

Hot Spots

We're taking a side trip here from the ears to the skin, but they're related concepts. The body has an inflammation which is coming to the surface and which should not be suppressed with antibiotics or steroids. The body needs to push the inflammation to the surface to heal it.

Hot spots are areas of inflammation which can come from a tick, a fleabite, a scratch, or a bite from another animal. The area gets moist, the hair gets matted down, the skin gets irritated, then the dermatitis spreads to a larger area.

You need to clip the hair really well, then wash with green tea or natural tea tree oil soap, then get all the soap residue off and dry it really well.

It needs to dry out, so do not apply a topical treatment like calendula gel. You can use **Hot Spot** from Natural PetRx, which is a combination of drying herbs.

Shirley Moore recommends **Hepar sulph**, which she says is a wonderful remedy she's used for years with great results (taken orally, like other homeopathics).

You can also support your animal with nutritional supplements like essential fatty acids, vitamin C and digestive enzymes.

Just be sure not to suppress the skin condition with conventional medication. Skin issues tend to come out where there is inflammation in the body – if it's in the neck and throat area, for example, it could represent a tendency to hypothyroidism.

Ticks and Fleas —
The Mighty Bites

Ticks are dangerous – because they carry Lyme and other diseases, and most ticks these days are infected with Lyme and/or several other serious diseases.

Flea *prevention* can be dangerous – commercial flea products contain toxic chemicals and should never be used.

Fortunately, holistic health care professionals have a whole different understanding of parasites that especially applies to fleas and also intestinal parasites.

I remember my first homeopathy teacher, Dr. Luc De Schepper, used to say that a healthy organism won't support parasites. Parasites are nature's way of thinning the herd: in a group of animals in nature, when one becomes weak and sick and starts to break down, parasites move in to hasten the breakdown and cull out the weak animal.

Pair that with the observation of Dr. Margo Roman and many other holistic vets I've talked to:

You can take an animal that's had fleas repeatedly, switch the animal to a raw foods diet with good supplements, and the animal is now resistant to fleas. Same animal, same environment, same exposure to fleas. No fleas. Well, maybe sometimes. But definitely more resistant.

What a different world-view! Did you know that even Pasteur, the "father of microbiology," said, "The microbe is nothing, the terrain is everything" – terrain meaning the host in which the germ (or parasite) is living.

Anyway, it's good news, because the commercial flea-killing products are really toxic and have never been tested for safety on humans. Think about it - they get on your pet's fur, you pat your pet, or worse still a child pats it, the toxic chemicals get on your hands and in your mouth ... totally not okay.

Commercial spot-on pesticides are so toxic, they should only be used as a last resort, when natural approaches have failed and there's a really bad infestation. (More info about spot-on pesticides in the **Resource** section, page 112). **Nux vomica** is a great remedy to use if you think your pet has been poisoned by flea and tick treatments or any medication.

If you give your pets healthy food and a healthy lifestyle, they should be free from fleas.

The exception would be a serious flea infestation, like moving into a flea-ridden house. Then you can use diatomaceous earth, a finely powdered natural mineral that's safe if you should ingest some. (When I owned a natural food store, we used to stir diatomaceous earth powder into the bulk grains to keep the moths out.)

You can call **FleaBusters**, www.fleabuster.com, to come and put the special powder into your carpeting and cracks in the floorboards. Or you can order the powder from them online and apply it yourself.

For your cats and dogs, if you've moved into the midst of a flea infestation, we recommend **Flea Free**, a flower essence from Green Hope Farms, www.greenhopeessences.com. You just put a few drops in their water bowl.

Or you can use a natural herbal spray with wonderfully fragrant essential oils like **cedar, lemongrass, rose geranium,** and **citronella.** Our favorite is

Quantum Spray with Fleabane from Earth Animal, and guess what, fleabane is an herb that repels fleas!

These sprays and the Tic Clip mentioned in the next section are available from Only Natural, a great source of natural products for your pets (www.onlynaturalpet. com). For the best prices, order through www.extrabux. com, an online shopping site.

Buck Mountain Parasite Dust is a good product to prevent BOTH fleas and ticks. It also works wonderfully to get them off your pet and out of your house during an infestation. It has diatomaceous earth plus herbs like neem and yarrow used traditionally to repel insects. www.buckmountainbotanicals.net

Taking **garlic, nutritional yeast** and/or **vitamin B-1** (thiamine) is another approach to repelling fleas and other insects. (In my natural food store, people used this combo to repel mosquitos.)

Ticks: Get a Grip . . .

What we just learned about parasites doesn't apply to ticks, unfortunately. No matter how healthy your pet, it won't grow a thick enough skin to repel ticks.

And ticks are hungry little critters! They may not have eaten for as long as two years. They can wait patiently on a blade of grass, waving their little legs, just waiting for your dog to come along.

Spot-on pesticides just don't work, the Lyme vaccine does not work well enough (there are many cases of vaccinated dogs getting Lyme), and it can have serious side effects. Much more about this (and how toxic they are) in the **Resource** section, page 112, but here's the condensed version:

Spot-on pesticides turn your pet into a walking No Pest Strip complete with toxic chemicals. They don't work because they don't kill the ticks fast enough – the ticks have time to inject the Lyme organism. Or the ticks can infect YOU by falling off your pet in your house (on your bed! do your pets sleep on your bed? of course they do and what are vets thinking, telling us we shouldn't let them, and who's the boss of you anyway?)

No getting around it – you have to check your pet for ticks several times a day during tick season (which is the first week in March through the first week in July here in Massachusetts). Take it as an opportunity to give your dog some good lovin', rubbing your hands through its fur.

Remember to check its head and ears and spots it can't reach – ticks seem to gravitate towards the places where your pet can't reach them.

If you find one, take it off with a **tick spoon**, a special device that has a slot that starts out wide and gets narrower so you can get a good grip to get the tick out.

Tweezers can leave the head behind (which may be busy injecting Lyme organisms into your pet - yuck!)

If no tick spoon, get a pair of tweezers and grasp the tick, quickly, as close to skin as you can. The longer you fiddle with the tick, the more time it has to lock its mouth parts under the skin. You can apply vaseline, which will make the tick weak and easier to pull off. Or you can use a cotton ball soaked with liquid soap. They suffocate the tick so it lets go. If the head is left it can cause an inflammation. Usually that will scab over and peel off.

After you remove the tick, clean the area with hydrogen peroxide, then apply a water dilution of **Calendula**.

If your pet does get Lyme, use the protocol on page 110 AND take them to a holistic vet. This is a serious, potentially crippling, even fatal illness. It may not show up at first; symptoms may develop over time. Even a dedicated holistic vet like Dr. Roman may need to use antibiotics to treat Lyme in some situations.

There's one more product you could try – **Tic Clip**. It is a German product that looks like a dog tag and emits an energy field, and they say it lasts two years. The best price we have seen is at www.extrabux.com, then go to the Only Natural Pet Store and you can get the product at a reduced price.

Intestinal parasites

Please follow your vet's standard protocol for deworming kittens and puppies, and for treating intestinal parasites. Dr.Roman finds that Strongid, the standard medication, is benign enough to recommend.

Heartworm

As long as we're talking about parasites . .

Dr. Roman says **cat heartworm** is so rare in New England that there's no need for preventive medication (apparently there are reports of it in the South).

For dogs, she recommends heartworm medication every 40-45 days, starting a month after you see mosquitos until a month after the first frost. Here in Massachusetts, that means June 1 – December 15.

This method does require returning for a test each year to make sure your dog is protected. But the test only costs what you just saved on medication, and this way you're putting minimal chemicals into your dog's body.

Dosage: To protect against heartworm only, use 1/4 the dosage of Interceptor (the same as the European product called Safeheart).

To prevent hookworms, roundworms and whipworms as well, use Interceptor in full dosage.

Prevention may be given every 40 days, as long as you will remember! So mark it on your calendar.

If you have small children in the house coupled with a dog that goes to a lot of kennels, parks, grooming facilities or play groups, you may want to stay on year round prevention like Interceptor just to insure against worms such as round worms that can be passed to children.

Rabies — The Original Vampire Story

You totally have to take rabies seriously – it is dangerous, even deadly, for your animal *and you*.

For your animal, there's a triple threat:

o   the *disease itself* is dangerous

o   as is the *vaccine*

o   and the *law*: your animal could be taken from you and euthanized IF it bites someone, IF that person files a complaint, and IF your animal is not up to date on its rabies shots – EVEN IF its bloodwork shows that it has antibodies to rabies.

So here's the deal.

The rabies virus is both fatal and sneaky – it takes over the brain of an infected animal and makes it want to bite other animals. Then its saliva transmits the disease along with the bite. Without the rabies vaccine, the first animal dies, all the animals it has bitten go around biting other animals, then they die . . . that's why it can cause an epidemic.

And don't think you're off the hook just because you live in a city. Urban wildlife like raccoons and skunks can carry rabies.

Nor are you off the hook if your animal is housebound. Bats are major carriers of rabies – a bat could get into your house and bite you or your animal while you are sleeping. The bite wouldn't show, and you wouldn't know!

Sound farfetched? It happened to a good friend of mine right here in Cambridge, Mass., where we like to think we are too civilized for such things, but a bat got into his little girl's room while she was sleeping. Since the bat could not be caught to test it for rabies, her doctor had to act *as if the bat did have rabies and had bitten her* – which meant a series of 7 or 8 shots for the little girl.

(That's the origin of the vampire legend, by the way – rabid bats biting people in the neck and giving them rabies is a real possibility. But then would the people don batwinged cloaks and go around biting others in the neck? That's the stuff of legends!)

So to get back to your cat or dog . . .
I remember once I was trying to protect my cat against too many unnecessary vaccines and wanted to postpone a scheduled rabies shot. Dr. Margo read me the riot act.

She told me horror stories of animals brought in by their unsuspecting owners to have a bite wound treated . . . the cat or dog had gone out and come back in with the bite, no idea how they got it . . . and the animal was not vaccinated against rabies …

Do you know what happens then?

The animal has to be quarantined for six months! and in some states that means isolated from everyone including you.

It could be that your animal actually *has* great protection against rabies, as good as if it were up to date on its shots, but that doesn't "count" in terms of the law.

Here's how we know if your animal is protected.
Holistic vets do **titers** for rabies (blood tests to check the level of antibodies). In general, vaccines are effective for years longer than the vaccine schedule would indicate.

Your animal could have an excellent rabies titer, indicating good protection against rabies. Note that the vaccine is only 86% effective (according to a recent study by Angell Memorial Hospital in Boston) – so the vaccine is no guarantee.

But the law at this point only recognizes vaccination status. It does not recognize titers.

Meanwhile, repeating the shot too frequently is dangerous! WHO, the World Health Organization, considers the rabies vaccine a carcinogen. Talk about being caught between a rock and a hard place!

So most holistic vets recommend the initial rabies shot plus the **legal minimum of a booster every three years.**

Here's one more thing to track:
it's called "**3-year status.**"

You can get a "pass" for three years (the annual rabies vaccine is not legally required) IF you get the first booster shot beween 9 and 12 months after the initial one.

But if you miss that 12-month deadline by even one day, you have to re-vaccinate your animal for rabies just one year later – giving your animal an unnecessary extra shot.

Story Time

Even way back in 1974, when Dr. Margo Roman was going to veterinary school and required to get two rabies shots, she was told she should have a titer taken every other year to see if the protection was holding, and "under no circumstances have another rabies vaccine if it is unnecessary because it can cause an auto-immune disease."

Can you imagine? Even back then, experts at a school of veterinary medicine knew that too many rabies shots could cause an auto-immune disease.

And doing a titer – checking blood levels of antibodies – was considered an acceptable way of checking protection, at least for vets.

Meanwhile, the "standard of care" in veterinary medicine continues to be rabies shots every few years, whether or not the animal needs it. And vets who use titers instead of shots for themselves are going along with the state laws requiring shots instead of titers for animals.

Not only that, Margo has done titers on herself for 36 years now – and she is still protected from that original set of shots from 1974!

She says that titers in animals show the rabies shot lasting for 7 years or longer.

If you would like to help vets trying to change the law to allow a healthier vaccine schedule, please go to www.rabieschallengefund.org.

Vaccines — Hold That Shot!

Do you know how vaccines work?
They stimulate your animal's immune system.

So what happens if you give vaccines against multiple diseases at the same time, year after year?

A couple of problems.

Overstimulating the immune system can cause an auto-immune disease - surprise! This makes sense when you think about it, and holistic vets in fact see it in practice.

They also see a connection between over-vaccination and cancer — for example, tumors can form at the vaccination site.

Here's another thing. Your animal's immune system is designed to create antibodies against invading disease organisms, and vaccines work by introducing those disease organisms (in killed form).

But injections are a totally unnatural way for your animal's body to encounter these organisms. Usually disease organisms pass through a series of barriers as part of the immune system — like the tonsils in the throat, or the enzymes in the digestive system.

Injecting several disease organisms at once is a further assault on the immune system. This is something that never happens in real life.

Plus, the injection contains a lot of toxic substances besides the virus, like aluminum hydroxide, which the World Health Organization considers a level 3 (out of 4) carcinogen.

So, bottom line – vaccines actually overwhelm your animal's immune system instead of supporting it. Animals that get vaccinated every year tend to be sicker and weaker than animals that don't.

(Of course, owners that spread out vaccinations are also likely to be feeding raw food and giving natural remedies and supplements, so it's hard to pinpoint one reason why these "all natural animals" are healthier.)

Perhaps the most poignant argument against vaccination that I've encountered is this:
Over-vaccinated animals tend to be more aggressive. Don Hamilton, DVM, in his wonderful book *Homeopathic Medicines for Cats and Dogs* (highly recommended!) cites an increase in aggression for a few days following a rabies vaccination. And he quotes an older vet saying that when he first started practicing in the 1950s, "animals were much nicer." The vet attributed the change in temperament to the increase in vaccinations.

So – what to do? Some diseases are deadly for our animals, and some vaccines are necessary.

A couple of things.

Only vaccinate for the diseases that your animal is actually apt to get. Some vaccines are for diseases only found in kittens and puppies – no need to vaccinate older animals.

Only do the absolute minimum vaccines necessary to protect your animal. How can you tell? Your vet can check **titers** (the blood levels of antibodies for each disease). They usually indicate that the protection is still robust and a vaccine can be postponed, sometimes for up to 10 or 15 years. Each animal is different, though – that's why you need to test.

Only do one vaccine at a time (only one shot at a time, and each shot containing only one disease organism). **Rabies especially should be given alone.**

Do not vaccinate an animal that is ill. This means cancer, an auto-immune disease, thyroid issues, any acute or chronic illness. Get a titer instead to make sure it is protected.

Give a remedy before and after the vaccine to protect your animal. **Thuja 30c,** a few pellets in the mouth right before and right after (or a few pellets in 4 ounces of water, stir well, splash a teaspoon on the gums).

Thuja works for all vaccines except rabies: give **Lyssin 30c** before and after the rabies shot. You won't find Lyssin in a store but you can easily get it online.

So which are the **deadly diseases** that even holistic vets vaccinate against?
Dr. Roman vaccinates for **distemper and parvo in puppies,** then titers older dogs.
She vaccinates for **panleukemia in kittens** and titers older cats.
If the titers indicate that the animal is not protected, then she would repeat the vaccination.

The puppy vaccine schedule is more complicated …

There's the **ideal scenario,** and then there's the **realistic** scenario.

The **ideal scenario** protects the puppy's immune system as much as possible, but it depends on circumstances that are hard to match:

You have to **have the mother titered** right before she gets pregnant. If she is protected against distemper and parvo (the diseases in question), the puppies will be born with protection. But in many cases you don't know the mother or her immune status.

You have to **keep the puppies away from other dogs** until they are 10.5 weeks old, the ideal time to give the first shot when the mother's antibodies are wearing off – but puppies are typically put up for adoption at 8 weeks or earlier, because they are so cute and adoptable then.

Finally, you have to keep mother and pups' immune systems healthy – with **raw foods and supplements**.

For example, Dr. Margo Roman had a dog titered before she gave birth, so she knew the puppies were protected. Then she allowed one of them to be adopted at 8 weeks – but the new 'parent' was a fellow holistic vet, and she knew he would follow the 'ideal scenario'. Here it is:

Parvo at 10.5 weeks; titer 6 weeks later and again 6 months later to make sure the antibodies levels have held up. (This can vary from dog to dog depending on circumstances, so don't assume that one shot is all your dog needs!)

Distemper at 13 weeks, titer as above.

If the dogs are shown (i.e. exposed to a lot of other dogs), **titer again every year.**

So the prerequisites are hard to fulfill.

In most cases Dr. Roman would recommend Dr. Jean Dodd's minimum vaccination protocol for dogs.

Dr. Dodd's website is www.hemopet.org.
This protocol is from www.itsfortheanimals.com:

Note from Dr. Dodd: The following vaccine protocol is offered for those dogs where minimal vaccinations are advisable or desirable. The schedule is one I recommend and should not interpreted to mean that other protocols recommended by a veterinarian would be less satisfactory. It's a matter of professional judgment and choice.

Age of Pups	Vaccine Type
9 - 10 weeks	Distemper + Parvovirus, MLV (e.g. Intervet Progard Puppy DPV)
14 weeks	Same as above
16 -18 weeks	Same as above *(optional)*
20 weeks *(or older, if allowable by law)*	Rabies
1 year	Distemper + Parvovirus, MLV
1 year	Rabies, killed 3-year product *(give 3-4 weeks apart from distemper/ parvovirus booster)*

Perform vaccine antibody titers for distemper and parvovirus every three years thereafter, or more often, if desired. Vaccinate for rabies virus according to the law, except where circumstances indicate that a written waiver needs to be obtained from the primary care veterinarian. In that case, a rabies antibody titer can also be performed to accompany the waiver request.

See www.rabieschallengefund.org for information about requesting a more humane rabies vaccine schedule.

Rescue Tales from Save A Dog

"I was at an event in which Save A Dog had a booth and a woman stopped by with her dachshund puppy cradled in her arms. She told me that the puppy had been lethargic ever since her vaccines a few days before.

"So I told her about how homeopathic **Thuja** is used to treat vaccinosis (the after-effects of vaccination). I quickly made her up a mixture of it and gave it to the pup.

"An hour later she stopped back at our booth to show me her pup, who was prancing happily along beside her. She thanked me at least a dozen times.

"Boy did that make my day!"

– Shirley Moore:

A great resource for understanding more about vaccines comes from the vaccine expert himself, Dr. Ronald Schultz. He spent his career working as an immunologist for a vaccine manufacturer, and now that he is retired he is able to tell the truth.

Dr. Schultz explains in a four-part interview on YouTube that there is no scientific evidence for annual vaccinations. He is interviewed by Dr. Karen Becker, the vet on Dr. Mercola's site (a great source of information about holistic health care for people).

Search YouTube for MercolaHealthyPets and then for the Schultz interview. You'll also find dozens of other informative videos by Dr. Becker.

Minimum Vaccination Schedule for Kittens

This is Dr. Roman's recommendation for a minimal vaccination schedule for kittens.

Keep the kittens isolated from large catteries or kennels.

Give the first shot when the mother's antibodies drop off, at 10.5 to 12 weeks.

If you can keep them isolated, just do one shot. If not, do two.

Do rabies alone, not with other shots. Wait to do rabies at 16 or 20 weeks, unless the cat is going outside and might be exposed to rabid bats.

Remember to keep the cat within the three year status described for dogs: be sure to repeat it within 9 to 12 months then the cat does not have to get another rabies shot for 3 years.

The standard recommendation for FVRCP is at 9, 12 and 16 weeks, then a booster at 1 year then 3 years.

She does only one shot, when the kitten is older, then titer to make sure the cat is protected . . .

unless the cat will be boarded, in which case it may need a booster at a year old.

If the cat is going outside in an area with a high rate of feline leukemia, then do two vaccines for it, separated them by at least a month, then do not vaccinate for it again.

For example: distemper at 12 weeks, the first leukemia shot at 16 weeks, rabies 2 or 3 weeks later, and the second leukemia shot 2 or 3 weeks after the rabies shot.

Cats should be screened for feline leukemia and feline AIDS.

Talking to Your Pet

You probably think I'm a tree-hugging nutcase. So, as with many of the other tips in this book, I'm going to suggest – just try it, it won't hurt, and it might work.

You might be surprised at the results. You just might need to adapt your communication style a bit to "animal-speak."

To illustrate, I'll give you a couple of examples from my life with my beloved pure white cat Princess. I used to travel a lot, and when I came home she would be sulking. She had a funny way of doing it – she would plant herself right in front of me with her back to me, and every now and then glance over her shoulder at me as if to say, "I am not talking to you. I am NOT TALKING to you. DO YOU HEAR ME?" It was hard not to laugh!

She would do this for a day or so and then forgive me and get over it. Then I learned from an animal communicator* to look at her life from her point of view – and how to handle it. Princess had been a stray, and every time I left, she went through abandonment trauma all over again. She had no way of knowing when I would be back, or even *if* I would be back. So she didn't know how she would get fed – and for Princess-the-foodie, meals were the center of her universe.

I learned this technique from the animal communicator. I call it the Vulcan Mind-Meld. I would hold her up and rest our foreheads together and then hold an image in my mind of my landlady from a cat's-eye point of view: my landlady's feet walking to my refrigerator and a bowl of food being placed in front of her. "Ella will feed you."

*Someone who has fully developed the ability to communicate with animals which we all have innately.

Then I would create an image of it getting dark. "I'll be away for one dark night," I would say, then repeat it for the number of nights I would be away. "Two dark nights. Three dark nights." Each time I would create an image in my mind of a dark night. Then she would be happy to see me, instead of sulky, when I got home!

Apparently animals are good at telling time – even the time of day. Princess used to run after me desperately as I rode my bike to my office, until I started saying, and transmitting, to her: "I will be back when it gets dark. I will feed you when I get back." Then she calmed down!

Towards the end of her life she developed a disturbing behavior: she began clawing at my eyes in the middle of the night while I was asleep. (I finally figured out she wanted water; she was heading into kidney failure.) It was frightening for me. I was afraid she would really injure one of my eyes. But I also didn't want to banish her from my bedroom in her last days.

So I transmitted to her "soft paws" and in my mind imagined her pawing at me with her claws retracted. I had learned from animal communicators that animals don't understand "not" or "no," as in "don't bark" or "don't run into the street." They just hear the command "bark" or "run into the street." So you have to find a positive substitute for the behavior you want to change.

Do you know, from that time on she started pawing me with gentle paws, no claws!

It works in reverse, too. Sometimes your animal seems to want something – they look at you intently and bark or wag their tails or somehow indicate you should follow them, but then you can't figure out what they want.

Sometimes you can understand them with a technique I call "Four on the Floor." You close your eyes and make your mind very calm. (This might be easier for yoga and meditation practitioners.) Then you imagine yourself down onto the floor looking at the world from a few inches off the ground. And you imagine yourself with fur and a tail. Then you imagine what it's like for them . . .

You might be surprised at the result, and at what simple workarounds you might find for a problem behavior! Like when I tuned into Princess and found that she could no longer jump onto my bed and needed a little box next to it. And here I thought she was boycotting me at night!

Another time, a very sad time, I was trying to puzzle out a big change in her behavior: she used to run to greet me when I came home, climb up onto my shoulders as I bent down to pat her, and ride up the stairs as if on a royal palanquin. Or if she were inside when I came home, she would be at the top of the steps waiting for me, her little ears perked in my direction.

Suddenly I noticed that she was now waiting for me on the porch and staring blankly in my direction, or, when inside, she would put her ears back and run away to hide under my bed. What strange behavior!

… until I put myself in her "paws" and realized . . . she was going blind (miraculously reversed by Dr. Margo).

If you would like to learn how to do this, I highly recommend Amelia Kinkade's *From the Horse's Mouth* and *The Language of Miracles*. Worth reading just for the stories alone!

And if your animal has a serious health problem, you may need a professional animal communicator to help tell you what is going on. Your holistic vet can probably recommend one – they tend to use them when diagnostic tests are inadequate for figuring out an animal's health problem.

Rescue Tales

The Story of Save A Dog
and Its Success with Natural Healing

Homeopathy For Rescued Dogs

Save A Dog was founded in 1999 by husband and wife team Shirley Moore and David Bernier of Wayland, Mass. After volunteering at local animal shelters and realizing the desperate plight of thousands of abandoned dogs, they founded the humane society and built a foster network so that the dogs they took in from local and remote dog pounds would have a temporary place to stay. Shirley and Dave would visit big city shelters and load up their van with many adoptable dogs, put them in foster homes, provide medical care and a holistic protocol, and made them available for adoption on their website, www.saveadog.org.

Medical care at Save A Dog was transformed after Shirley had a dramatic cure with homeopathy. Shirley spent five months unsuccessfully trying conventional medications to treat the ringworm she developed while doing post-Katrina search and rescue work in New Orleans. One application of Boiron's Thuja Cream cleared up the ringworm in three days!

Shirley was impressed – and she realized that if homeopathy could work as well on dogs, it could transform medical care at Save A Dog. She embarked on professional training at Teleosis School of Homeopathy and learned that, in fact

o Animals respond really well to homeopathy

o It costs much less than conventional treatment, saving the shelter thousands of dollars a year in medical costs

o It's so safe that the treatments can be administered by adoptive parents and volunteers o It's so simple that these folks can easily learn how to use remedies for their dogs

o Using homeopathy and other holistic methods leave dogs healthier overall, unlike conventional medications which can compromise the immune system.

Save A Dog's holistic protocol includes:

o probiotics and supplements in the dogs' food to boost the rescued dogs' immune systems

o animal healing music and aromatherapy to help them heal from the emotional trauma of losing their homes

o homeopathic remedies for intestinal upsets and other health problems that plague rescued dogs.

Shirley's mission has now expanded: to teach other shelter operators this holistic approach. A shelter recently contacted her about an epidemic of upper respiratory infections that was plaguing their cat shelter. Shirley sent several homeopathic remedies and a copy of Dr. Don Hamilton's *Homeopathic Medicines for Dogs and Cats*. The result? An email: "It's a miracle!" The staff were amazed at how fast the remedy stopped the epidemic. "It's so quiet in here!" they said.

This book is the first step in spreading this approach to shelters nationwide. Please consider donating a copy to your local shelter, if they are interested, and tell them they can order it from us in bulk to provide to their adoptive parents (available at www.greenhealing.org).

Save A Dog is a privately funded organization and relies entirely on donations to keep the rescue mission going. Please consider donating: www.saveadog.com.

On the following pages are some success stories from Save A Dog.

Bitsy is a tiny 3 year old Yorkie who was helped tremendously by homeopathy after her spay surgery. Her small size combined with a history of many litters made for a very painful spay surgery for this six pound dog. When the anesthesia wore off she cried out in pain.

A few drops of **Staphysagria** was all she needed to fall back asleep. It would last for a few hours, then she would wake up whimpering and another dose put her back into the comfort zone.

She finished with **Arnica** for the bruising and soreness around the incision and recovered very quickly.

Blossom was a pup who developed agoraphobia following her rabies vaccine. She was terrified to go outside and especially of open spaces. She would run for cover and hide in the bushes. She was given **Lyssin**, then three days later she had a major breakthrough and was no longer fearful of the outdoors.

Lyssin is the nosode (special remedy) associated with rabies. We usually use it before and after a rabies vaccine but it can also be used to treat other conditions. In the old days before the vaccine, homeopaths used it to *treat* rabies.

A ten week old Lab pup named Little Girl was showing symptoms of a bee sting at her foster home and she had all the signs of an allergic reaction. In the short drive over to my house, the puppy's eyes became swollen shut and her face was swollen to at least twice its normal size. She was lethargic and panting. The plan was to take her to an emergency vet hospital but she was in such bad shape, I was afraid she would die on the way.

So I gave her the remedy **Apis** and the swelling went down in five short minutes! If there weren't witnesses in the room, I wouldn't have believed my eyes.

Little Girl then squirmed out of her foster mom's arms, jumped down and drank a whole bowl of water, went outside, peed, and came back in, prancing around in celebration of her miracle. We were all so amazed and thankful – we cried tears of joy. This simple remedy saved the puppy's life.

A litter of 8 week old puppies broke with the parvo virus, one by one. The first puppy was taken to an emergency veterinary hospital where she was put on an IV and given antibiotics. Lack of funds plus a poor prognosis from the vet hospital prompted me to treat the other puppies at home with homeopathy.

The next pup broke with a sudden 107.5° fever. She was red hot with very bloodshot eyes, so we gave her **Belladonna** and subcutaneous fluids. Her fever dropped by one degree per hour over a four hour period! The next morning she was up, wagging her tail, and looking for something to eat – that is unheard of, because parvo can be absolutely devastating.

The next puppy broke with different symptoms, so I used a general flu remedy, **Baptisia**, and he did really well on it. The remaining pups were treated with remedies matching their symptoms.

All were eating within 24 to 48 hours and they were significantly larger than the puppy who was treated at the ER hospital. When the conventionally-treated pup returned, she was anemic and still needed additional support before she fully recovered. In fact she always looked like the runt after that. The homeopathically-treated pups were robust and eating heartily in less than a week.

One of the 'parvo pups'

Freddy is Shirley's dog and her pride and joy. He is a Hairless Chinese Crested who developed necrosis to his left ear flap. At first it had the appearance of ringworm, but was unresponsive to Thuja and the tissue around the flap started to die off quickly.

In desperation, we took the suggestion of a vet who performed surgery to trim the ear and remove the dead tissue. This was a tough lesson to learn in our early years of practicing homeopathy, because the necrosis picked up where it left off and started to eat away at a much shorter ear flap. After much searching through homeopathic books, we gave him a dose of **Mercurius solubilis** 200c and voila, the necrosis stopped!

Freddy is ten years old now and his favorite pastime is to run around terrorizing the bigger dogs in his household!

Can you see the indentation in Freddy's ear, on the left, where the tissue was necrotic (dying off)? Freddy on the right, after cure. What a cutie!

Resource Guide

New Dog Instructions...96

Holistic Protocol for Shelter Dogs 103

Directions for Mixing Homeopathic Remedies 106

Giving a Pill to a Cat 109

Quick Guide to Homeopathic Remedies 110

Why Give Probiotics to Dogs 111

FAQ Sheet on Lyme Prevention...............................112

Preventing Lyme with the Lyme Nosode 116

Natural Dewormer 118

Recommended Reading 120

Recommended Suppliers...124

Recommended Websites..125

Find a Practitioner 126

About the Authors..127

Save A Dog informational handout (excerpts)

New Dog Instructions

Food: Your dog should be on a high quality food so that he grows and develops a strong immune system. The best diet is a fresh foods (raw) diet, but if you choose to feed a commercially prepared diet, try to incorporate a little fresh food along with the dry kibble. When selecting a commercially prepared food, try to select a grain-free food. Especially avoid corn-wheat-gluten ingredients and never buy food listing "by-products" (which are downed cows, road kill and even euthanized pets). The better quality food (human grade is preferred) you feed your pet, the less you will have to spend on his vet care later in life. We recommend a diet of fresh food, or home cooked meals supplemented with probiotics and supplements.

We do not recommend commercial pet food. For the truth about this food, see www.truthaboutpetfood.com. They have a weekly email newsletter with updates on pet food recalls and other news.

Preventing kennel cough, even giardia: For large adult lab-sized dogs, one tablet of grapefruit seed extract in their kibble every morning will help boost the immune system (it sells for $5 at Vitamin Shoppe) as it's known for its strong antioxidant qualities. Continued use of grapefruit seed extract is strongly recommended to maintain good health and even prevent giardia. For more information on the benefits of grapefruit seed extract, see /www.pureliquidgold.com.

Heart worm preventative. Heartworm pills are a monthly heartworm preventive that you can only purchase with a vet's prescription. Collies and mixed breed Collies and Australian Shepherds are very sensitive to Ivermectin, so do not use Heart Guard on these breeds. See www.vetmed.wsu.edu/depts-VCPL for more information. Interceptor is preferred by most vets because it also acts as a wormer against several kinds of worms. Since most shelter dogs are prone to parasites, we recommend ongoing worming, and Interceptor helps with that. The heartworm preventives reach back 4 months from the time your dog is exposed, so every other month is more than often enough to give Interceptor once your dog's stools tests negative for worms. I recommend giving it every other month in case the dog throws up the pill unbeknownst to you. That way you're doubly covered too if he did ingest It.

Flea and tick preventative. We do NOT recommend using any flea/tick drops that contain pesticides. You do not want pesticides in your dog's blood stream. Most of the flea/tick manufacturers are being investigated by the government (see www.epa.gov/opp00001/health/petproductseval.html).

When should you call the vet? If your puppy has loose stools, it could be caused by change in diet or the excitement of being in a new home. Any diarrhea that persists for more than 24 hours or diarrhea that is accompanied by vomiting should warrant a visit to the vet.

To locate a holistic vet, see www.ahvma.org. If you have a young pup, it is always wise to use a traveling vet so that you don't expose him/her to diseases like kennel cough or parvo.

For loose stools, canned pumpkin or slippery elm in the food works great too. Best to feed a bland diet if your dog has an upset stomach. See www.holvet.net/slippery_soup.html for more information and helpful hints.

Spaying/neutering: If your pup is not altered, please spay or neuter your pup well after the vaccinations are completed, preferably in adolescence so that the dog's development is not short-circuited by premature removal of much-needed hormones. www.caninesports.com/SpayNeuter and www.mmilani.com/commentary-200509 are helpful articles. If you're adopted pup was spayed/neutered too young, it will help to give beneficial hormones, see www.estrapet.com.

Acclimating Your Rescued Dog Into Your Home

Getting your new dog/pup home safely: Before bringing your new dog home, check your house and fenced in yard (if you have one) and make sure there are no holes or gaps where your new dog can slip through. Bring an ID tag to clip to your dog's collar (Save A Dog provides its own ID tag, but not all shelters do). Prior to leaving the premises, attach your dog's ID tag onto your dog's collar. We usually carry the dog to the car unless the dog is well leash trained or too heavy. Still, even the best trained dog can panic when getting into an unfamiliar car, so precaution is always taken.

It is best to go straight home to acclimate your dog to his new environment before night fall. If you have a light-weight leash, it's best to use that leash, even in fenced in areas. The first few days you can have them drag the leash so that you can safely bring your dog inside. Many southern dogs are not accustomed to stairs, so you may have to carry him/her inside the first few times and subsequently use treats to coax your dog up the stairs.

What to expect the first 24 hours: The first day can be very exciting for a dog and you may find that s/he is not that hungry. This is not unusual. Please make sure you allow quiet time for your pup so that s/he can eat and rest, especially if you have kids. This can be in a crate or in an area of the house that is safe, i.e., gating off the kitchen.

For adult dogs, it is not unusual for them to "hold their water" (urine) for a few days. We've had dogs who have not have a bowel movement for up to four or five days. Once your dog relaxes, things will start to move internally and they should begin having normal bowel movements.

It is not unusual for house-trained dogs to have an accident in a new environment. Also, male dogs will often lift their leg on furniture the first day. It doesn't mean they're not housebroken, but it means they're "marking" their new home as their own. It is wise to confine a new dog and to limit access to rooms other than the kitchen or small rooms with tiled floors. Puppies who are paper-trained will often view a scatter rug as the same as a piece of paper so roll up the rugs.

Adjustment Period. Please allow for an adjustment period for your new dog, especially if the dog has recently spent time in a shelter and has suffered many losses and a disruption of his former life. It is not uncommon for these dogs to suffer from separation anxiety in the first few weeks and months in the new home, especially as they are eager to attach to their people.

It is also common for the new dogs to become protective of one or more members of the family. This is why it is of utmost importance to have a trainer lined up from day one.

Trainer Resources. Training is required for all adopted dogs. You can find a professional trainer on the web site http://apdt.com/ and click on Search for Trainer. Another web site is www.clickertraining.com. Dogwise.com is a great resource for dog training books and videos. The Web site http://www.apdt.com/ has a list of certified trainers.

Getting Your Puppy or Dog on a Schedule. It's important to set a schedule for the puppy as soon as possible, so that house training is easy.

1. First thing in the morning, take the pup outside to go to the bathroom. Give lots of praise when she goes, and promptly bring her in for breakfast.

2. Feed your puppy. Within 10-20 minutes take her outside again as she will often need a bowel movement shortly after eating. Feed in the crate as this provide another opportunity for a positive experience in the crate. Do not allow her to free feed. The reason is that you want her on a schedule so that she will not have unexpected bowel movements. Dogs who eat all day tend to "go" all day.

3. Once she's had a bowel movement, praise her and bring her in to play. She should be good for another hour or so. When you cannot supervise your pup, you should put her in the crate with a chew toy to keep her busy. Puppies can generally "hold it" for an hour or two, so when the hour is up, take her out again and praise her when she goes. You'll want to take him out before you retire for the night and then again first thing the next morning.

Crating at night will help teach your pup to hold it through the night. If she whines in the middle of the night, it may mean that she has to go. Do not put the crate in your bedroom as dogs are light sleepers and tend not to sleep through the night if in a bedroom. Put them in a family room or kitchen, in the crate with an absorbent towel in case of accidents. You can put a night light in the room, play soft music. After a few minutes the pup should settle down.

Socialization. It is very important to socialize your dog. This is the time to have lots of friends over, including men, women, and children. If your dog is from a rural area, you need to gently and slowly socialize him and not put him into crowded situations or walk them on busy roads where noises may startle them into a fearful response. For adult dogs, daily walks will keep them socialized with pets and people. It's important that your dog meet new dogs on a daily or weekly basis. Even if you have a fenced-in yard, walking your dog is needful for socialization.

If you have children in the family: It is not a good idea to let the puppy on the furniture as elevation equals status and the dog needs to be kept at a lower status than the children. Also, no tug-o-war or anything playing with hands around the puppy's face as that will encourage nipping. Keep a chew toy handy to redirect any play biting and if all else fails, give a short time out.

Microchip: Should you microchip your dog? We're not so sure anymore. See www.ChipMeNot.com for information on cancer forming where the microchip was placed.

Save A Dog informational handout

Holistic Protocol for Shelter Dogs

Shelter dogs have an urgent need for a holistic protocol as soon as they come into our care. Most have a heavy load of parasites, have been assaulted with chemicals to combat fleas, and then are given the full range of vaccines, and are put under anesthesia for spay and neuter surgery. This onslaught of chemical warfare on the already compromised immune system can wreak havoc on the dog's health. Our protocol is to build them up as quickly as possible in the short time-frame in which they are in our care. Prior to adoption, we educate the adopter regarding a holistic protocol ongoing. We also provide additional holistic and homeopathic counseling at no cost to the dog's adopter.

The following is the protocol we use at the Save A Dog shelter, but you can tweak this according to your experience and comfort level, if you operate a kennel or animal shelter.

o   Assess the dog's overall physical and emotional needs upon arrival.

o   Give Rescue Remedy and homeopathics like Aconite to frightened dogs.

o   Build the dog's immune system with vitamins and probiotics. Vitamin C in the AM and probiotics for the PM feeding (probiotics work at night). Pawiers is the best vitamin therapy you can use. We are a distributor, but retail stores are catching on too.

o   Use homeopathic remedies to clear vaccine damage (Thuja, Silica, Nux vomica) o Use Optique Eye Drops by Boiron for "goopy eyes" or eye infections.

o Switch to a high quality kibble, adding lots of enzymes to minimize intestinal disturbances. Every feeding is an opportunity to add supplements.

o Add supplements to the kibble, with a splash of organic low-sodium chicken broth to dissolve the herbs and enhance the flavor.

o At first sign of infection/illness, give Aconite 30c. This is also a good remedy for frightened dogs. At first sight of cough, runny nose or fever, give 1 dose of Aconite 30c. It usually nips illness in the bud.

o Herbal spray of lavender and chamomile (get the essential oils in natural food stores) will calm down barking dogs in the kennel. Rescue Remedy works great as well.

o For loose stools give slippery elm from Whole Foods or Mountain Rose Herbs (a fabulous herb supplier).

o Homeopathic remedies for diarrhea are Arsenicum, Veratrum, Podophyllum. You have to look up the particular symptoms to match the right remedy. (Or see information on probiotics on page 111.)

o Follow vaccines with a dose of homeopathic Thuja. See directions for giving remedies.

o Give a dose of homeopathic Staphysagria (instead of rimadyl) following spay or neuter surgery. It works wonders. Also, Arnica reduces bruising and swelling and is good for pain as well.

o Use the Lyme nosode (Borrelia burgdorferi 30c) or Ledum instead of Lyme vaccine to prevent Lyme disease.

o Puppies get New Zealand Colostrum and probiotics

every day. Probiotics work at night so give in the PM feeding. Give powdered Vitamin C in the AM feeding.

o   Follow Dr. Dodd's vaccine schedule for puppies. Page 80 in this book or www.wellpet.org/vaccines/dodds-schedule.htm. Dr. Dodd's website is www.hemopet.org/. She has saved many puppies from the deadly parvovirus, including Oprah's puppy. She's a great resource.

Save A Dog informational handout

Directions for Mixing Homeopathic Remedies

Mix the dry pellets* into purified or distilled water and syringe it into their mouths, or shake it up and squirt some into their water bowl.

Directions: Tap 2-3 pellets of the remedy you're going to use into a bottle containing 4 oz. of spring or distilled water. Let the pellets dissolve for about 5 minutes, then shake vigorously and give the bottle a couple of thwacks on your open hand.

Give 1cc (1/4 tsp) directly into your pet's mouth. You can always pour a little in an empty cup or bowl for him to drink (after shaking or stirring the mixture) or put a capful into your dog's water bowl, but not for a cat as cats tend not to drink from the bowl. You can use a syringe for either, such as the small syringes used to give medications to babies. You need a different syringe for each remedy although you can keep reusing it for that remedy - maybe label it with a marker.

Administering remedies. Give the remedy on a clean palate, i.e., no food should be in his mouth. You don't have to give it on an empty stomach, but just no food in his mouth so that it will absorb more quickly. Do not mix in their food as it won't work.

If you can't get the pellets out of the tube, hold it vertically with the clear plastic lid on the bottom and twist the cap firmly, which will pop a pellet out with each twist. You might need to peel off the little paper sealing strip, or it might come off when you twist the cap.

Storing remedies.

1. Store them in a cool dark place, away from strong-smelling substances such as eucalyptus, camphor, oil of cloves, Vick's vapor rub and aromatherapy oils. It is not a good idea, therefore, to keep them in the bathroom.

2. Do not store remedies near mobile phones, televisions, microwave ovens or computers. The fridge is okay.

3. Ensure the lid is well secured after use.

4. Do not store where there is direct sunlight, or excessive heat or cold.

5. Don't transfer remedies from one container to another.

6. After a few weeks, toss the remedy out and you can reuse the bottle for other remedies.

Most remedies that are mixed in water last about 2 weeks. If you want them to last longer, use distilled water and add 10 drops of vegetable glycerine and store in the fridge. Our pre-mixed remedies include the glycerine.

Where to buy homeopathic remedies

Whole Foods, or any natural food store (although they only have 30c)

Homeopathic Educational Services,
www.homeopathic.com

www.elixirs.com

Additional Information from Dr. Margo Roman

Giving nutritional supplements: Only mix supplements in regular dinner when you are sure the pet will eat them. We don't want to discourage your pet from eating well. As treats to mix meds in, things that have a strong smell usually work best. Sardines, dark tuna in oil, and liver are very popular. Some people have success with peanut butter, cheese balls, yogurt and cream cheese. You may also try baby food in jars.

Giving your dog a treat first that does not contain the medicine will often lower their guard enough to get them to gobble the next morsel. Some clients have had success making a liver or sardine "frappe" that contains the day's supplements and syringing it in.

Giving homeopathic remedies: The homeopathics (i.e. Thuja, Arnica, Ledum etc.) can NOT be given in food, so your best bet is to just splash the dose on your pet's gums or lips. Homeopathic remedies are absorbed through mucous membranes, so a quick splash and you're done. Do not give food to your animal 20 minutes before or after giving your remedy.

Begabati's method for giving a pill to a cat

o   Wrap the cat tightly in a towel so the paws are trapped.

o   Place the cat on the floor and crouch over it - one knee on each side, pinning the cat firmly (but not putting any weight on the cat).

o   Place one hand on the cat's head: the three middle fingers on top of the head, the thumb and little finger on each side of the lower jaw.

o   Tilt the cat's head upwards — that makes it more likely to swallow.

o   Use the thumb and little finger to pry the cat's jaws open.

o   Quick! Whip the pellet into the cat! Then hold its mouth shut so it can't spit it out!

o   Stroke the cat's throat to encourage swallowing.

o   Tell your cat that she is absolutely the best cat in the world and your absolutely most favoritest cat. Actually you need to do this on a daily basis. Cats need to be addressed in superlatives. They thrive on it. Plus, as I used to tell Princess' ladies-in-waiting (i.e. her kitty sitters), she was on "a special diet of a million kisses a day." Kisses, treats and lots of praise help the pill go down!

Dr. Roman recommends a "**pill pusher**" or **"pill gun**." They have a soft tip that holds the pill and you quickly push it into the back of the cat's throat. But that assumes you can open the cat's mouth . . . so you still might have to use the towel method above!

Quick Guide to Homeopathic Remedies

The name on the bottle is likely to be longer than the nickname we use in this book. Here we'll give the full name to avoid confusion, with the nickname highlighted in **bold**.

Also, each remedy can do many things, and only one of its uses will be listed on the label on the bottle. Here are the main remedies in this book, and a few of the main uses for each:

Aconitum napellum: fright, sudden onset e.g. of fever
Arnica montana: bruising, soreness, post-surgery
Arsenicum album: vomiting, diarrhea, anxiety, restlessness
Belladonna: aggression, sudden high fever
Bellis perennis: after abdominal surgery
Bryonia alba: joint pain when it hurts to move
Calendula officinalis: cuts, lacerations, incisions, wounds
Calcarea **carb**onica: bone and joint problems
Calcarea **phos**phorica: healing broken bones; osteoporosis
Carbo vegetabilis: collapse, difficulty breathing
Hypericum perfolatum: injuries to nerve-rich areas
Ignatia amara: sudden grief, emotional upset
Ledum palustre: puncture wounds, tick bites, Lyme
Lyssin: protection from the rabies vaccine; rabies-like behavior
Mercurius solubilis or vivus: ear infections
Natrum muriaticum: silent grief
Nux vomica: vomiting, diarrhea, other digestive problems
Phosphorus: bleeding, post-anesthesia
Podophyllum peltatum: fire hydrant diarrhea
Rhus toxicodendron: stiffness in the joints; poison ivy
Ruta graveolens: injury to tendons, ligaments, periosteum
Silica: push out splinters; gum irritation
Staphysagria: following spay surgery
Sulphur: chronic skin problems
Symphytum officinale: fractures
Thuja occidentalis: vaccination protection; ringworm, fungal
Urtica urens: hives, rashes

Save A Dog informational handout

Why Give Probiotics to Dogs

Probiotics are a must for dogs and especially recommended if people are considering switching their dogs to the raw diet. Probiotics are gut-friendly living bacteria that are found naturally in a healthy digestive tract.

They can be found in food such as yogurt, although they are not numerous enough in yogurt to colonize the guts of animals effectively. High-quality powdered supplements in powdered form are more effective for therapy as they are far more concentrated. Each teaspoon contains literally millions of good bacteria.

Probiotics improve the health of the digestive tract by changing gut acidity, aiding digestion, and helping to detoxify harmful substances. They boost the dog's immunity and actively produce antibiotic substances. They are particularly crucial for dogs who have been on a poor diet and for stressed dogs. They are also helpful after the use of antibiotics, steroids, or anti-inflammatory agents.

o   Probiotics may be useful in chronic skin disease, allergies, arthritis, cystitis, candidiasis, colitis, irritable bowel syndrome, and some forms of cancer (Chaitow and Trenev, 1990).

o   Diarrhea: supplementation can help rebalance the population of bacteria that are affected by acute and chronic diarrhea.

o   Before switching a dog to the raw diet, it is recommended that you build them up on probiotics first.

Probiotics work at night, so it is best to give in the PM feeding. At Save A Dog, we give all kenneled dogs probiotics in every afternoon feeding. We use **RxBiotics** in powdered form.

FAQ Sheet on Lyme Prevention

The ticks are out in full force so I [Shirley Moore] have been doing some more research on the best and safest preventive measure against Lyme disease. I've come to the conclusion that homeopathic **Ledum** is the best defense against Lyme disease (for dogs and humans alike).

Will topical "spot-on" pesticides prevent Lyme? No. Spot-ons will not prevent Lyme. They don't repel ticks at all and the tick still delivers the spirochete before it dies.

But why does my vet tell me that spot-ons prevent Lyme? In laboratory tests the tick takes 48 hours to infect the dog. The premise is that the tick will die before it has a chance to infect the dog. More proof is coming out that ticks we're encountering in the wild deliver the spirochete faster, hence the "spot-on protected" dogs are contracting Lyme disease. It makes perfect sense that wildlife is more robust in its natural environment than in a laboratory. Historically, we've seen many dogs with Lyme disease who have had the spot-on products applied, both with the Save A Dog volunteer's dogs as well as in the general adoption community.

Is there anything I can put on my dog to keep the ticks off? There's not much in the way of benign drops or sprays as most contain pesticides. It is a known fact that pesticides cause cancer. Therefore, in my opinion, using spot-on products is like burning your house down to get rid of ants. Read your ingredients as there are some oils and herbs that will deter ticks. Pennyroyal and rose geranium are good natural tick deterrents.

Is there something I can put in my dog's food to keep the ticks off? Yes. **Garlic and brewer's yeast** are well known for keeping the bugs off of dogs. The combination is safe and it's been used for years. You can buy it in a tablet or get it in a powder from most natural food stores.

Check the website www.holisticpetinfo.com, and under Conditions look for Immune Support. It's a helpful web site, and they also sell **Moducare,** which is touted by holistic vets as building the immune system against Lyme and other diseases. **Astragalus** is also well known as a good defense against Lyme disease as it builds up the dog's defense system against Lyme.

What can I give my dog after they've been bitten by a tick? A really good defense against Lyme disease is homeopathic Ledum. Homeopathy strengthens the vital force and is very successful at curing diseases of the blood as well as chronic diseases. For a human, take one homeopathic pellet of Ledum 30c twice a day for 2 days following the tick bite. For dogs, give the same dose of Ledum 200c. Since dogs aren't as able to dissolve a pellet on their tongue, you can dilute it in 4 oz of distilled water, once the pellet dissolves, stir briskly, and give 1cc or several drops on the dog's tongue. Discard the water after the second day.

What about the homeopathic nosode?

The homeopathic nosode made from the Lyme spirochete (Borrelia burgdorferi) has been used successfully to prevent as well as treat Lyme disease. (A nosode is a homeopathic remedy specifically for a particular disease.) It's wise to use the nosode to prepare yourself or your dog when the ticks are not biting. See the following handout on Lyme prevention and treatment. The same nosode can be used in a 200c potency to treat Lyme, but you should work with a homeopath as the dosage needs to be monitored.

No preventive is 100% effective, but the Lyme vaccine is only 34% effective and has side effects. The nosode is gentle enough not to have side effects and is widely known for its effectiveness. Since it does not guarantee immunity, you need to keep giving it on schedule throughout tick season.

A good example of the success of homeopathic nosodes was demonstrated during a lepto outbreak in Cuba recently after a hurricane swept through the country and they were in short supply of the lepto vaccine. Nosodes were instrumental in eliminating lepto. For more information, see http://homeopathyresource.wordpress.com/2009/01/01/ successful-use-of-homeopathy-in-over-5-million-people-reported-from-cuba/. It is a good article on the effectiveness of homeopathy versus traditional vaccination on more than 2.5 million people.

What if my dog has Lyme disease? If your dog has Lyme disease, you should work with a homeopath as the treatment is individualized depending on a number of things, one being the advancement of the pathology. This will determine the course of action. At the very least, ask for a C6 test so that you can get a baseline of the number of antibodies in the dog's blood. This will be your yard stick for determining if the disease is progressing or is on its way out of the body. Dr. Stephen Tobin, a holistic vet in Connecticut, has successfully treated thousands of dogs and horses. He advises giving the dog Ledum 1M three times a day for three days in a row. See http://cassia.org/ledum.htm for a copy of Dr. Tobin's very informative article plus information on how to find Ledum 1M.

What about giving the prescribed antibiotic?

More information is now coming out that the antibiotic prescribed for Lyme does not stop the disease from progressing. It seems to lower the number of antibodies for awhile, but Lyme disease progresses nevertheless. Many homeopaths agree that doxycycline and other antibiotics will prevent the immune system from fighting the disease, so it's a double whammy. The numbers look good for awhile, but it comes back with a vengeance. Shirley Moore has personally seen this over and over with friends' and volunteers' dogs, and with people too. Also, since the Lyme spirochete confers no immunity, once a dog has Lyme, they can be reinfected every time exposed. Once you treat for Lyme, you have to wait six months before having another C6 blood test done.

Save A Dog informational handout

Lyme Prevention with the Lyme Nosode

If you have a dog that has never been exposed to Lyme disease, for example, a dog new to a Lyme-epidemic area or a new puppy, then you can prevent Lyme with the Lyme nosode, Borrelia burgdorferi 30c. A nosode is a special type of homeopathic remedy that is specific for a particular disease. Nosodes are not available over the counter. You can get Lyme nosode from elixir.com.

As with any homeopathic remedy, you can either put the pellets directly on your dog's tongue or mix it in distilled water. The advantages of mixing in distilled water:

o it's a little stronger that way,

o you don't have to worry about whether or not your dog has spit the pellet out or not, and

o it's a good way to get more mileage out of your bottle of homeopathic pellets (especially ones that you have to special-order).

Mixing instructions for homeopathic dry pellets:
Tap 1 or 2 pellets into a bottle containing 4 oz. of spring, filtered or distilled water.
Let the pellets dissolve for about 5 minutes, then shake vigorously and give the bottle a couple of thwacks on your open hand to activate the remedy.

How to give the nosode:
Squirt 1cc (1/4 tsp.) directly onto the dog's tongue (do not mix with food). You can use an eyedropper if you want.

Give on an empty palate, no food in his mouth, but your dog can have food 10 minutes before or after administering the remedy. It is not really affected by food, but it needs to go on a clean tongue.

How often to give the nosode:
It's best to start before the tick season.
To start, give one 1cc (1/4 tsp) for 3 days in a row.
Wait one week, then give one dose per week for 4 weeks. Then give once a month during tick season.
The following spring, have your dog tested for Lyme.

What if I run out of the nosode?
If you run out, or if the remedy starts to get cloudy, you can simply wash the bottle in hot soapy water or run it through your dish washer and make a fresh bottle.

Remember there is no 100% guarantee
Although Shirley has had success using the Lyme nosode for Lyme prevention on her rescued dogs, she says that there is no guarantee of 100% immunity when it comes to Lyme disease. The vaccine only confers 34% immunity. Even if a dog has had Lyme disease, the tick doesn't confer immunity against future cases of Lyme.

Remember to consult a professional if your dog does get Lyme
When treating Lyme disease, it is best if you work with a trained homeopath because advanced cases of Lyme may require additional treatment and closer monitoring.

Save A Dog informational handout

Natural Dewormer

Before reaching for that bottle of womer, why not try homeopathic **Cina**? For dogs and cats you give it in a 200c potency. For birds, 30c potency seems to work just fine.

Any worming should be done at two week intervals. It usually take 3 separate doses (2 weeks apart) to completely rid the worms from your dog or cat. One dose is a few pellets.

Cina 200c is available at homeopathic.com or elixirs.com. 30c is available in natural food stores.

(Note that this is an entirely different remedy from China – it's not a typo.)

We find that this natural deworming protocol works but only if the adoptive parents can remember to repeat the remedy three times.

Editorial comment: If you want to use a commercial dewormer, please use Interceptor instead of Heartguard Plus. It has recently been named in a lawsuit by a whistleblower — a former employee who was the manufacturer's former head of "global pharmacovigilance" and who alleges that the manufacturer knew Heartguard was losing its effectiveness.

Apparently this was especially problematic in the Mississippi Delta region where mosquitos are plentiful, since heartworm is carried by mosquitos, and dogs treated with Heartguard were developing heartworm.

Rescue Tales from Save A Dog

I wormed a large Mastiff with **Cina 200c** because I didn't want to have to pry open the mouth of such a large dog and risk getting chomped on. So I mixed up 2 pellets of the Cina 200c in distilled water, dissolved, stirred briskly, and put a half teaspoon in his water bowl.

The next day when I came in there was a long note from a new volunteer describing the many different kinds of worms that were in the dog's stool that morning!

From that point on I was careful to write in the log if I wormed a dog with Cina, so there would be no surprises.

—*Shirley Moore*

Recommended Reading

The top books we recommend getting right away:

Pitcairn, Richard. *Dr. Pitcairn's Complete Guide to Natural Health for Dogs & Cats.*

Hamilton, Don. *Homeopathic Care for Cats and Dogs.*

Lennihan, Begabati. *A Healer In Every Home: QuickStart Edition.* The "people version" of this book. Lots of useful info that applies to pets too. Using the remedies for yourself will help you to understand better how to use them for your pets.

Additional resources for holistic health care

Brennan, Mary. *Complete Holistic Healing for Horses.*

Day, Christopher. *Natural Dog Care.*

Elliott, Jill. *Whole Health for Happy Dogs.*

Fougere, Barbara. *Pet Lover's Guide to Natural Healing for Cats and Dogs.*

Fox, Michael. *The Holistic Dog Book: Canine Care for the 21st Century*

Frazier, Anitra, and Norma Eckroate. *The Natural Cat: The Comprehensive Guide to Optimum Care.*

Goldstein, Martin. *The Nature of Animal Healing.*

Goldstein, Robert and Susan. *The Goldsteins' Wellness and Longevity Program: Natural Care for Dogs and Cats.*

McCutcheon, Paul, and Susan Weinstein. *The New Holistic Way for Dogs and Cats*

Messonier, Shawn. *The Natural Health Bible for Dogs and Cats.*

Rasmussen, Jan. *Scared Poopless: The Straight Scoop on Dog Care.* (This is Begabati's favorite new book. If you like *A Healer In Every Home,* you'll really have fun with *Scared Poopless!)*

Schwartz, Cheryl. *Four Paws Five Directions.*

Stein, Diane. *Natural Healing for Dogs and Cats.*

Tilford, Greg. *Herbs for Pets*

Volhard, Wendy. *Holistic Guide for a Healthy Dog*

Walker, Kaetheryn. *Homeopathic First Aid for Animals*

Whole Dog Journal and *Animal Wellness* magazine

About the dangers of vaccinations and commercial pet food:

Jordan, Patricia. *The Mark of the Beast* (on vaccines)

Martin, Ann. *Food Pets Die For* and *Protect Your Pet: More Shocking Facts*

O'Driscoll, Catherine. *Shock to the System: The Facts about Animal Vaccination, Pet Food and How to Keep Your Pets Healthy.*

Making healthy pet food

Taylor, Beth and Karen Shaw Becker. *Dr. Becker's Real Food for Healthy Dogs and Cats*

Training

Barney, Carolyn. *Clicker Basic for Dogs & Puppies.*

Patricia McConnell and Karen London.
www.dogwise.com
Play Together, Stay together
Cautious Canine
The Other End of the Leash, and all her videos

Pryor, Karen. *Don't Shoot the Dog.* (a classic)

Pellar, Colleen. *Living with Kids and Dogs without Losing your Mind.*

Fisher, Gail. *The Thinking Dog: Crossover to Clicker Training.*

King, Trish. *Parenting Your Dog.*

Sternberg, Sue. *Out and About With Your Dog – Dog to Dog Interactions on the Street, on the Trails, and in the Park.*

Randy Grim & Melinda Roth. *Don't Dump the Dog – Outrageous Stories and Simple Solutions to Your Worst Dog Behavior Problems.*

Animal Communication

Bekoff, Marc. *The Emotional Lives of Animals.*

Kinkade, Amelia. *From the Horse's Mouth* and *The Language of Miracles.*

Hiby, Lydia. *Conversations with Animals.*

Smith, Penelope. *Animal Talk, When Animals Speak, Animals in Spirit,* and more.

Schoen, Allen. *Kindred Spirits.* (about human-animal relationships)

Dr. Roman's animal communicator is Marcia Zais at Heart to Heart Communications, www.marciazais.com.

Begabati's is Rae Ramsey, www.ramseycommunications.com

Great videos about using homeopathy at home

If you'd like to learn more about homeopathy and you'd rather watch/listen than read, we highly recommend the Mastering Natural Remedies series from Miranda Castro. They're about people homeopathy but the same concepts and same remedies apply to pets.
Miranda is a colorful and entertaining lecturer, full of memorable stories. You don't actually need to watch; you can mostly listen while multitasking.

Homeopathy 101 (first aid, recovery from surgery, etc.)

Stress Busters (remedies for common stressors, physical as well as mental and emotional)

avalable on www.greenhealing.org

Recommended Suppliers

Homeopathic Remedies

Any natural food store will have the most common remedies in a 30c potency (strength)

For stronger potencies, and more unusual remedies:

Homeopathic Educational Services,
www.homeopathic.com

www.elixirs.com.

Herbs

Mountain Rose Herbs, www.mountainroseherbs.com

Essential oils

Wellington Fragrance
www.WellingtonFragrance.com/Essential-Oils/

Flower essences for animals

GreenHope Farms, ww.greenhopeessences.com

Spirit Essence, www.spiritessence.com.

Natural foods and supplements

Only Natural, ww.onlynatural.com

To get the best prices at Only Natural, go through
www.extrabux.com

Recommended Websites

Dr. Mercola's site about natural healing
www.drmercola.com, highly recommended,
mostly about people, and it has a
newsletter from a vet, Karen Becker DVM
http://healthypets.mercola.com/sites/healthypets/
You can subscribe to it at
drkarenbecker@mercola.com
and see Dr. Becker's informative videos on YouTube
(search for MercolaHealthyPets)

Dr. Roman's sites:
www.mashvet.com has informative articles
www.drdomore.com has previews of her documentary

Dr. Marty Goldstein's site, www.drmarty.com

www.whole-dog-journal.com and
www.dogs4dogs.com (the *Scared Poopless* site!)
www.dogwise.com has a wealth of books, videos, and
tools for the new dog adopter. We strongly recommend
their Puppy Kindergarten DVD.

www.**TruthaboutPetFood.com,**
www.PetsumerReport.com
you can also subscribe to Susan Thixton's newsletter:
email Support@truthaboutpetfood.com

Advice on **feeding raw to cats:**
www.rawfedcats.org
www.littlebigcat.com, Dr. Jean Hovre's site

Shirley's Wellness Cafe (for both people and animals)
www.shirleys-wellness-cafe.com/healthypets.htm

Find a practitioner:

American Holistic Veterinary Medical Association
www.ahvma.org has a directory of holistic vets and
several articles on holistic home care

Acupuncture
The American Association of Veterinary Acupuncture
www.aava.org

Chiropractic
American Veterinary Chiropractic Association
www.animalchiropractic.org

Herbalist
Veterinary Botanical Medical Association www.vbma.org

Homeopathy
The Academy of Veterinary Homeopathy
www.TheAVH.org

The National Center for Homeopathy
www.nationalcenterforhomeopathy.org
lots of info, geared towards people, applies to animals

Educational Opportunities
The College of Integrative Veterinary Medicine
in Australia, offers on-demand courses internationally,
some only open to vets, others to the public
www.civtedu.org

About Shirley Moore

Shirley Moore is the President and Founder of Save A Dog, Inc., a Massachusetts-based dog rescue and adoption agency incorporated in 1999. Her work has been so outstanding that she received the first American Red Cross Award for Animals.

Shirley and her husband, Dave, have fostered and placed for adoption many puppies and dogs from all parts of the country. Shirley has attended workshops on dog training and canine behavior, and for years she taught classes in dog obedience and Puppy Kindergarten.

Following her remarkable cure from ringworm with a single dose of a homeopathic remedy (described on page 88), Shirley decided to study homeopathy as a way to treat the dogs arriving from shelters in the South, where they would have been euthanized. The dogs would arrive frightened, malnourished, and loaded with fleas. Shirley spent three years in training as a professional homeopath at Teleosis School of Homeopathy in addition to attending numerous seminars on veterinary homeopathy.

As a result, she has transformed her medical treatment of the dogs in her care. Right from the first weekend of her homeopathy training she was seeing remarkable cures like the 'parvo pups' described on page 93. She has also trained hundreds of volunteers in homeopathy and holistic methods. (Many of them are teens, and Shirley jokes that she is training the next generation of holistic vets!) She now teaches workshops on homeopathic first aid and "How to Get Your Dog Off Drugs."

Reaching out even further, Shirley is now responding to requests from other shelters for advice on treating their animals holistically. (Word is spreading that shelters can heal their animals more quickly and save substantially on medical costs with a holistic approach.) She recently took four of her teenage volunteers on a mission to five shelters in West Virginia, where they donated homeopathic remedy kits and taught the shelter staff how to use them.

She has learned that taking a holistic approach in assessing dogs for adoptability is the best way to do right by the dog and has trained her staff to take this approach as well. Assessing the dog is important as well as assessing the home in which the dog will flourish. It's just as important to have the dog on a good diet with the right supplements as it is to train the dog. Therefore, her volunteer staff, as well as her adopters, are educated in both modalities. A holistically minded adopter is most often the best choice for dogs who have been over-serviced by well-intentioned vets, but every dog will flourish on a holistic protocol.

Puppies are her specialty, as she has personally fostered many litters and has kept in touch with their adoptive families. She enjoys doing the puppy consultations as it's a wonderful way to help people and their dogs avoid problems down the road as the dog enters adolescence. She realizes that most people only have a puppy once or twice in a life time so she is happy to share her knowledge and provide the necessary hand-holding during those first few crucial weeks and months.

Prior to founding Save A Dog, Shirley and her husband Dave Bernier met while working together in the high tech industry. Shirley left a career as a manager in the high tech industry to pursue her dream of saving dogs. She has developed and managed multiple departments in the area of technical publishing and Web development in the high tech industry and has used her business knowledge and entrepreneurial skills to build the all-volunteer organization.

Dave works as a software engineer and also serves as a director and the technical guru for Save A Dog. For the first ten years of its existence, Dave and Shirley ran Save A Dog out of their home, with Dave providing the financial support — for which Shirley and thousands of dogs are eternally grateful.

They are also very grateful to Dr. Margo Roman, who is Shirley's vet and who has taught Shirley so much. Begabati is grateful to both Margo and Shirley who, as students in her homeopathy school, taught her about using homeopathy for animals.

Shirley doing animal rescue work after Hurricane Katrina.

About Margo Roman, DVM

Margo Roman, D.V.M. is owner of M.A.S.H. - Main Street Animal Services of Hopkinton in Hopkinton, Mass. (www. mashvet.com), which she established as a full service Veterinary Clinic in 1983. In 1993, she expanded into an Integrative Veterinary Practice and in 2001added a new "green" and environmentally balanced Holistic Health Care Center.

Dr.Roman graduated from Tuskegee University, School of Veterinary Medicine in Alabama in 1978. She was the first female vet to graduate from the International Veterinary Acupuncture Course in 1976. During the same year she did her Externship at the Animal Medical Center in New York City. Dr. Roman's internship was at Angell Memorial in Boston, MA from 1978-1979. She was a member of the faculty at Tufts University's Veterinary School from 1979-1987. Her desire to find as many options to help animals stay healthy has led her to taking extensive coursework in Homeopathy, Acupuncture, Chiropractic, Herbs and Botanicals and other integrative modalities.

Dr. Roman has spent years of study at the Renaissance Institute of Classical Homeopathy with Dr. Luc De Schepper. She has also attended Dr. Pitcairn's advanced homeopathy courses for several years. Dr. Roman also took classes at Teleosis School of Homeopathy and courses at Tufts Veterinary School in Acupuncture, Advanced Herbal Medicine and Veterinary Chiropractic.

Dr. Roman has always had an interest in Natural Health. Her parents were very health and environmental conscious. Because of her love for animals, she wanted to be a veterinarian from early childhood. She would bring injured or lost animals home and care for them until they were able to be re-homed.

Dr. Roman has been politically involved in W.A.N.D. (Women's Action for New Direction) and has lobbied extensively locally and in Washington, D.C. as a grass roots activist on peace and environmental issues.

With a desire to educate and empower animal caretakers to know about options in health care for their companions, Dr. Margo Roman collaborated with filmmaker Simone Hnilicka to produce the Dr. DoMore Documentary preview (see www.drdomore.org). The 2009 version was produced from over 800 hours of film footage of more than 175 doctors, professionals and animal caretakers. Millions of views have been seen on the internet and in presentations around the world.

Dr. Roman and Hnilicka established the nonprofit Center for Integrative Veterinary Care with the Integrative Health Pet Expo in 2009 (www.ihpe.info). The newest endeavor is the Dr.ShowMore Calendar 2011, which had 14 veterinarians modeling for a *Calendar Girl*-like *au naturel* educational piece. This calendar was sold internationally and raised funds for the documentary, student scholarship and tsunami relief in Japan. It even went to Thailand, where her presentations on Integrative Veterinary Medicine in the U.S. allowed her the opportunity to treat the Thai Royal Family's cat with Acupuncture and Homeopathy.

Dr. Roman has lectured nationally at AVMA, NAVC, AHVMA, Wild West, and internationally in China, Japan, Thailand and Canada. She wrote a chapter in *Small Animal Ear Diseases* by Lou Gotthelf (2000), and in *Integrating Complementary Medicine into Veterinary Practice* 2009 by Goldstein, Palmquist, Broadfoot, Wen, Johnston, Fougere and Roman.

Dr. Roman has been a board member of the American Holistic Veterinary Medical Association and the Peace Abbey in Sherborn, MA. She is a member of

o   the American Veterinary Medical Association

o   Massachusetts Veterinary Medical Association

o   Academy of Veterinary Homeopathy

o   International Veterinary Acupuncture Association

o   Veterinary Botanical Medical Association

o   American Association of Ozone Practitioners

o   National Center for Homeopathy

o   Integrative Medical Association

o   the Medical Collaborative Working Group at Massachusetts General Hospital

o   Green Sustainable Committee in Hopkinton, Mass.

Margo Roman and her husband Jeffrey were married in 1979 and have three children: Shira, Noah and Dalia; two standard poodles Geneva and Lilihana; and a cockatoo Saffron. They share their green solar home that they built in 1981, way before it was the trend.

About Begabati Lennihan

Begabati was born into a medical family: her father, a vascular surgeon, ran a vascular research lab where he tested the prototype model for the Doppler ultrasound device. Her mother was a research biochemist who researched stains for Dr. Papanicolau while he was developing the Pap smear. (Her mother's promising career came to an untimely end with the arrival of Begabati; her mother had a second career later in life as a nature-loving third grade teacher.)

Her parents were also early conservationists and Audubon enthusiasts. When Begabati was 8, they had landscapers create a wildflower garden for her in the back yard, complete with a map with the botanical names of all the plants. (To her delight, these same plants showed up later in her life as medicinal herbs and homeopathic remedies.)

Begabati entered Harvard in 1969 planning to become a doctor like her dad, but she developed a passionate commitment for natural healing as an undergraduate, and her life took a different turn. At a time when there was no professional training in natural medicine, she graduated from Harvard in the top 1% of her class and, in a truly unusual career move, opened a health food store.

Begabati ran her health food store until she was 40, interacting with thousands of customers and developing a treasure trove of knowledge about natural remedies – from her studies and, more importantly, from talking to customers about what worked for them and how they could tell.

Turning 40 and determined to pursue professional training in natural healing, she chose homeopathy as by far the most effective of the modalities in her health food store. She was impressed by both the speed of its action in acute cases and the depth of its reach in chronic cases. It could resolve trauma from the person's early childhood, and it could heal emotional problems in a way that vitamins and herbs could not.

Begabati co-founded the Renaissance Institute of Classical Homeopathy in 1996 with her mentor, the internationally-distinguished homeopath Dr. Luc De Schepper. She served as administrator of the school until 2001, while it was in Boston. She was Director of Teleosis School of Homeopathy, a professional training program, from 2003 to 2010.

In 2010 she turned her focus to educating and em-powering a wider audience in basic home health care with natural remedies, by founding the GreenHealing Institute. She also practices classical homeopathy at the Lydian Center for Innovative Medicine in Cambridge, Mass.

Mostly, though, she likes to teach and to share what she knows. She has been appointed a Health Expert to answer questions on Dr. Mehmet Oz's ShareCare website. You can see her passion for natural healing in action in her community-access TV show, *A Healer In Every Home,* on YouTube (GreenHealingTV channel).

Begabati has been blessed with five cats in her life – her childhood cat Kitt-I … Queenie, the slightly neurotic cat she inherited from her landlady … her beautiful beloved pure-white Princess … and now the twins, Sammy the BoyCat and Misty the GirlCat.

Her unusual name ("Beh-GAH-buh-tee" meaning "a fast-flowing river") comes from her spiritual teacher, the late Sri Chinmoy, who — in addition to being an internationally-distinguished peace advocate — loved homeopathy and loved his little dogs.

CPSIA information can be obtained at www.ICGtesting.com
Printed in the USA
266149BV00002B/3/P